Making a
DEAL
THE ART OF NEGOTIATING

by

Martin Teplitsky, Q.C.

Lancaster House

Lancaster House
17 Dundonald Street, Suite 200
Toronto, Canada
M4Y 1K3
©1992

Canadian Cataloguing in Publication Data
Teplitsky, Martin.
Making a deal. The art of negotiating.
ISBN 0-920450-04-0

1. Mediation and conciliation, Industrial.
2. Arbitration, Industrial.
I. Title.
HD5481.T46 1992 331.89'14 C92-095449-9
Typeset, printed and bound in Canada

To my parents, Jack and Ida,
with whom I first
learned to negotiate

TABLE OF CONTENTS

CONCLUSION

INTRODUCTION

My own experience in "making a deal" comes from twenty-five years as a lawyer specializing in litigation. For practical purposes, because very few cases ever find their way into a courtroom, most of that time has been spent in negotiating settlements. As well, for the past seventeen years, I have practised as a mediator and an arbitrator, helping others to settle their disputes. Finally, when I was a full-time academic at Osgoode Hall Law School, the subject of "negotiations" was part of my advanced course in civil procedure.

While the principles discussed in the pages which follow apply to all negotiations, the context of the discussion concerns the negotiation of labour-management disputes. Here, it is important to understand that, while labour legislation across Canada obliges unions and employers to bargain in good faith, this requires no more than that each party accept the legitimacy of the other, and that both parties engage in rational discussion of the issues with the intention of reaching a collective agreement. The requirement to bargain in good faith merely sets the stage. It does not dictate the techniques of bargaining, nor does it provide the impetus to settle. These derive from a consideration of the alternatives: the threat of strike or lockout or, in the case of essential public services, the prospect of compulsory arbitration.

I assume throughout this book that the parties are bargaining in good faith in an effort to conclude a collective agreement. The principles I recommend will help you to achieve that result. In the bargaining that I have witnessed, problems are created largely by inexperience and lack of knowledge, not by bad faith. Should you encounter bad faith, your remedy lies with the Labour Board.

During the course of labour-management bargaining, you will be involved as a negotiator in three separate and distinct relationships: first, with your own principal; second, with the negotiator for the other party; third, with a neutral, i.e. a conciliator, fact-finder, mediator and/or arbitrator. Success in negotiations requires that each of these relationships work effectively. I will explain the negotiator's duties and responsibilities in each of these relationships and the tactics necessary for success.

I will also set out some principles which I consider essential if you wish to negotiate successfully, as well as various techniques you may use and tactics you may encounter. At the same time you should never lose sight of the fact that, sooner or later, almost every dispute is settled. The trick is to accomplish this goal sooner rather than later.

This book is designed to help you achieve more satisfactory settlements in a shorter time frame and with less anxiety. It is intended to be a practical work. There are no footnotes or references to other texts or articles, for the reader would not be advantaged by a display of academic learning in support of the ideas which I am presenting. I believe my suggestions will work for you. If you try them, take credit for your successes and blame me for any failures. As a neutral in labour disputes, I am used to being blamed.

1

The Key to Negotiating

DON'T GO ON A FROLIC OF YOUR OWN

It is an unfortunate fact that many negotiators do not understand their role. Negotiators should never forget that they are negotiating on behalf of someone else, not for themselves. They are "agents", not "principals". As agents they have a duty to be honest and direct in their dealings and to provide their principals with the information necessary to give appropriate instructions. In a labour-management context, the principals are the employer and the employees in the bargaining unit, and it is for these parties that the negotiators toil. They are not negotiating on their own behalf.

This simple point has important consequences. The negotiator's task is to obtain a settlement which the principal will consider reasonable. Your job as a negotiator is not to please yourself. It is not your ego needs which are to be served. Success as a negotiator depends upon your accepting this principle.

NEGOTIATING IS NOT A WIN/LOSE GAME

The desire to "win" arises naturally in a society as competitive as ours. Unless you are aware of the desire to win, you can never control it. It is like greed. Moreover, it is seductive to rationalize your desire "to win" as a desire to do the best for your principal. The greatest excesses can always be explained by any agent on the basis that he or she was only trying to achieve the best for his or her principal. There is also the risk that you may infect your principal with the "I must win" disease. Your reward will be a party who is never satisfied with the result.

Very often, I witness negotiators risking the loss of a satisfactory bargain by pressing for demands which would not make the package significantly more acceptable even if achieved. The negotiation has become a "game" which they want to win. They will settle only if they think that they have won. This common attitude leads to the prolonging of disputes, the development of antipathy between the parties, and ultimately to confrontation.

What these negotiators forget is that their principals are not interested in "games". They want a fair settlement which is made quickly. They do not want the uncertainty of delays, or the inconvenience and cost of confrontation and litigation. These negotiators do not realize that their principals will not appreciate the petty gains which constitute the "win" even if they are aware that these have been achieved. Their principals are never likely to be ecstatic about the bargain. It is trite to say that a good bargain is one which both sides are somewhat unhappy with. What people do appreciate, as I have said, is a fair settlement which is quickly achieved. If you are looking to win, you will be a menace as a negotiator and should switch to bridge or squash.

THE "BEST DEAL" SYNDROME

Another version of the "I want to win" sickness is "I want to get the best deal". The evil in this attitude is less obvious. It is, however, in effect, a rationalization of "I want to win". Of necessity, if I achieve the best deal, the other team is getting the worst deal. I am winning and they are losing.

This objective is particularly destructive because it sets you up for an impossible task. It is a modern version of the quest for the Holy Grail. You will never know when you have the best deal. There is no way to tell. There is no one to ask. The "best" admits of only one acceptable result and that result can never be known.

As a negotiator, you should be satisfied with a reasonably fair settlement. When you seek a reasonable and fair settlement, this involves a range of acceptable results. If you seek the best, you will always be disappointed, because you will never know that this has been achieved. The quest for the best results from the insecurity that affects all perfectionists.

Although you should disabuse yourself of this foolish notion, recognizing its presence in others will help you to plan strategy and tactics to ensure that they believe that they have achieved the best results. For example, most settlements are concluded in the wee hours of the morning, largely to create the impression that the parties have exhausted themselves in holding out for the "best" settlement. One can make a fair and reasonable settlement any hour of the day or night. It is only the "best" that will deprive you of a night's sleep. The post-midnight settlement is also used as a mechanism for manipulating one's principal. It is more difficult to criticize a negotiator who has been bargaining for 36 hours straight and who has stayed up all night to get the job done.

A major stumbling block for many negotiators is their inability to recognize what is fair and reasonable, that is, to recognize when they have done a good job. Often, when I mediate, negotiators say to me: "But, look at what I am not getting in this settlement". I tell them: "If you measure your success in life by what you do not accomplish, you will always be a failure". No one achieves all of his or her goals. In fact, smart negotiators leave something on the table. This means that they don't nickel and dime. Why? Because they understand the stock market maxim: "Sometimes the bulls win, sometimes the bears win, but the pigs always get slaughtered"!

THE PERILS OF WIN/LOSS

These attitudes—"winning" or "getting the best deal"—are particularly harmful in any situation where there is an on-going relationship such as in collective bargaining between labour and management. Let us assume that you win in a particular negotiation and they lose. You got the best deal and they got the worst. What will your reward be for this achievement? You will have made the other team very upset. You will have made them look foolish. They will be embarrassed. Naturally, they will try to get even. Getting even can take all kinds of forms. Unwritten understandings may no longer be respected. Favours formerly done will now be refused. Co-operative working relationships will be destroyed. You will have to bargain again in a year or two. You can imagine what a joy that will be.

One reason negotiators have difficulty in evaluating their success is that they measure the results on a round-by-round basis. Negotiators often change in each round of bargaining, and it may be difficult for them to have a longer term perspective. However, in an on-going relationship, success must be measured across a continuum of collective bargaining. If you have the longer term in mind, it takes the pressure off each round of bargaining, so that it does not become a life and death situation. After all, because of changed economic circumstances or other factors, any particular settlement may turn out to miss the mark. You can make it up in the next round of bargaining. One year you may be at the low end of the range of reasonable, the next year at the high end, and so forth. With this attitude it will be much easier for you to conclude your negotiations.

On the other hand, repeatedly making settlements either at the low end or the high end of the range of reasonable will cause problems in the relationship because one of the parties will either be receiving too little or be paying too much. It is easy to make small adjustments. It is more difficult to correct a significant "falling behind" or to bargain large "clawbacks". If your last contract missed the boat, make sure that you get back on board at the first opportunity. Regrettably, I have witnessed many situations where one party received a "windfall" in a particular set of negotiations and then was unwilling to make adjustments in the next round of bargaining. When a party perceives the contract as "out of line", anger and resentment are sure to follow. You should be prepared to recognize the legitimacy of the other party's interest in correcting the inequity. Unwillingness to do so can have lasting repercussions.

THE WIN/WIN APPROACH

This is a matter of ordinary common sense. The other negotiator will never make a deal if there isn't something in it for his or her principal and if it does not appear that by making such a deal he or she is doing a good job. In reality, most bargaining strategies are designed to create the impression that there is something in it for the other team and that they are getting a good deal. Moreover, a "win/win" attitude is obviously suited to an ongoing relationship. How to achieve the perception of "win/win" is a technique that is essential to the art of negotiating effectively.

The perception that the other party has of the proposed settlement usually depends on two factors. The first is its assessment of the alternatives to settlement. This is crucial. Will it do better or worse down the road if there is no settlement? If better, will it be sufficiently better to run the risk of not settling? Settling offers security. Not settling offers ulcers.

Second, the other party may measure the value of the proposed settlement in terms of the extent to which your demands have been reduced in the course of bargaining. Realistically, the reduction of demands does not provide a very sound basis for assessing the worth of a settlement because it is always a simple matter to reduce demands considerably if they are inflated in the first place. Nevertheless, in my experience, negotiators are influenced by this factor. It is a selling point with their own principals that they have achieved a significant reduction in your demands through their negotiating skills. Starting out with your bottom line robs the other side of any sense of gain.

SELLING THE DEAL

Whatever strategy a negotiator chooses, it must be designed to address two objectives. First, to secure the desired settlement. Second, to satisfy the other party that it has accomplished something positive. Unless you achieve the second objective, it is not likely that you will achieve the first.

However, parties will settle a dispute only if they believe that they are better off doing it now as opposed to later. A party will not settle if it is persuaded that more can be achieved later. Awaiting developments—pattern-setting settlements, changes in economic conditions—may appear to be sensible. Moreover, postponing decision-making is a common human trait.

But the wait-and-see attitude is the enemy of a settlement, and your job is to undermine this attitude. Your role as a negotiator is to persuade the opposite party either that it is better to settle now or that waiting will not create an advantage. In other words, achieving a settlement *now* requires that you satisfy the other side (and your principal) that *now* is the *right* time and that the bargain is the *right* bargain. You can point out the risk that the anticipated developments may be disappointing. In this regard, you have certain levers at your disposal. After all, waiting increases the anxiety level of the parties. Most people crave certainty.

However, you will not be able to allay the parties' concerns if you do not know what they are thinking. You must find out. How? By asking questions. When a reasonable settlement offer is not selling, you are entitled to suspect that the other side has developed a "reason" to wait. The same applies when your own principal is reluctant to conclude a reasonable deal. Find out what is bothering the parties. Then talk them out of it!

2

You and Your Principal

INTERACTING WITH YOUR PRINCIPAL

As a good negotiator it is vital that you relate effectively to your principal. Indeed, this skill may be the most important that any agent needs. When I was a very young junior lawyer, the senior partner in the firm told me that the only thing wrong with being a lawyer is having clients. This apparently paradoxical statement reflects the reality that relating to one's principal is very difficult. You must sort out preferences, establish priorities, obtain a sensible mandate, avoid unrealistic expectations, deliver what you promise, and then pray that your principals will accept the bargain you recommend. Few people realize that what is most appealing about becoming a judge is that you lose all your clients.

Moreover, the more principals you represent, the more difficult your task. Your principal may be a committee, council or board, composed of several members. Their views will not always be the same. You must work with them to achieve a consensus. It is not possible to bargain effectively if you are not clear as to the bargaining goals. If the committee is a large one, it may be important to identify the individuals with real influence. If you can persuade them, they will usually persuade the group.

This is not always an easy task. The person who talks the most may not exercise real influence. I recall one mediation in which I assumed that a particular member of the management bargaining committee, because of his important role in the organization, had the power required to sway the committee. I decided to meet with him to enlist his aid in support of my mediation effort. What I discovered was that he had no power, resented the fact, and because of it was determined to frustrate any settlement.

TRUST IS A TWO-WAY STREET

Because your relationship is one of agent and principal, the law imposes upon you the duty to act honestly vis-à-vis your principal, to keep your principal fully informed, and to act in your principal's best interests. It is vital, too, that you have the trust of your principal, and the confidence that nothing is being held back from you. This is not always to be taken for granted. Your principals may not necessarily share their thoughts with you. Some will trust you, others will not. And some will attempt to manipulate you by holding back their bottom line positions and concealing their true objectives.

Your principals can tell what they want, even what their preferences and priorities are, but only you can advise them whether or not their expectations are realistic and whether they can be achieved. In my opinion, it is better not to undertake a negotiation for a principal whose expectations are unrealistic. It is not sufficient to say: "You are being unrealistic. I cannot achieve these goals". Your actions speak louder than your words. If you accept the assignment, your principal will think that, regardless of your words, you believe that you will be able to accomplish the goal. No one undertakes the impossible. In the end you will have an unhappy principal.

Therefore, it is vital at the outset that you honestly tell your principals what they can reasonably expect from the negotiations. If you express your opinion as a range, you will have some latitude in making the bargain. You are not then tied to only one perfect result.

DON'T RAISE FALSE EXPECTATIONS

It is a dangerous practice for a negotiator to promise more than he or she can hope to deliver. In order to secure the assignment it may seem advisable to appear confident and aggressive and to promise fantastic results. These aggressive promises will come back to haunt you. Your principal will remember every extravagant statement you make. Some may even remember statements you did not make. You must avoid falling into this trap. Be honest. Be balanced. Do not promise more than you can deliver.

As a mediator, I have frequently observed the following sequence of events. At the outset, the negotiator makes sensible and reasonable predictions about the negotiations. However, as often happens, matters do not proceed according to plan. The negotiation is not proceeding smoothly. The other party is obdurate and refuses to make concessions. Delay is mounting. The principal is complaining. To placate the irate principal, you promise more. You up the ante. Instead of 5%, you now say you will get 6%. What were once throwaways are now sacrosanct. This is a formula for disaster. When a reasonable deal does emerge, you will not be able to make it because your principal's expectations are now unreasonably high.

What should you do when your negotiations are going poorly? First, your principals will not blame you if the other party is unreasonable. They will blame you if you do not keep them apprised of the state of bargaining. Report frequently and tell the truth. Explain the lack of progress. If material circumstances have changed since you obtained your mandate, ask for a new one that is more realistic. Devise a plan to overcome the roadblocks in the negotiation. Tell your principal about your plan. Do not make promises you cannot keep. If necessary, move quickly toward a confrontation. Remember that some people will settle only at the courtroom door or when a confrontation is about to begin.

Do not be afraid. Your principals will accept the truth, even if the message is different from what they would have preferred. We underestimate the readiness of people to accept the truth.

NEVER LOW BALL YOUR PRINCIPAL

Some negotiators consider it prudent to "low ball" their own principals. In effect, the negotiator reduces the principal's expectations below the level that is reasonably achievable. By this tactic, the principal is grateful for a normative result and is conditioned in advance to accept it readily. The principal will also believe that the negotiator has done a wonderful job. To illustrate, suppose you believe that a reasonable settlement would be in the 4-5% range. You advise your principal that you think that you can achieve 3-3.5%. Then you finally produce 4%. As a negotiator, you are a hero and the principal can't wait to sign on the dotted line.

For my own part, I do not approve of this kind of manipulation. It is unethical. An agent owes his or her principal the duty to be honest. This form of manipulation requires that you lie to your principals. Moreover, this approach is a very cynical one. It assumes that if you tell your principals the truth, they will not be able to make an intelligent choice. It assumes that you are "superior" and in a paternalistic way must protect your children (the principals) from themselves.

However, although the distinction is a subtle one, there is nothing wrong in seeking instructions to settle at 4%, even though you believe it is possible to obtain slightly more, as long as you do not jeopardize the 4% settlement in the course of trying to improve upon it. When you produce 4.75% your principal will be pleased.

ASSESSING THE RISKS

As a negotiator it is important to weigh the risks before advising your principal on a course of action. It is also important to share these risks with your principal, who otherwise cannot make an informed choice. You must be conscious of the influence you exert on your principal, through the opportunity you have to describe and evaluate the risks. Otherwise, it will not be the principal who makes the necessary choices. It will be the negotiator who leads the principal down a predetermined path.

Consider this example. Your principal has the right to proceed to interest arbitration if negotiations fail. The other side has proposed a wage increase of 5% to settle the contract. You are asked by your principal what the chances are of obtaining a better result at arbitration. If you advise that in your view you think it is probable that the arbitrator will award 4-5% (if you represent the union) or 5-6% (if you represent the employer), it is obvious that your principal will accept the offer. If you advise that in your view it is probable that the arbitrator will award 5-7% (if you represent the union) or 3-5% (if you represent the employer), it is equally obvious that your principal will reject the offer and proceed to arbitration.

You must be prepared to make a sound assessment of the risks. You should give your honest opinion. I emphasize that this should be done at an early stage. Although the ultimate decision is not yours, your principal is relying on you and is dependent on your advice. If you waffle in order to avoid any possibility of being wrong, your principal will be unable to make a decision. But beware of misguided optimism. One frequently has the sense that matters are undertaken with high hopes of success and ultimately solutions are forced on a party only after the negotiator develops a sudden awareness of risks. It is natural to fall in love with your side before the battle begins.

As a negotiator you must be careful not to impose your own agenda on your principal. Your personal views are irrelevant, and it is irresponsible to fight a crusade on the back of your principal over an issue that is of little importance to the principal. You should not proceed without your principal's consent and, just as with a surgeon advising a patient about the risks of an operation, it should be informed consent. It is neither proper nor fair for professionals to use their control over risk assessment to manipulate their principals' decisions.

No course of action involves a guarantee of success. If you exaggerate the magnitude of the risks, you can encourage a settlement. If you minimize their magnitude, you can ensure that there will be no settlement. What to do? Strive to present a balanced opinion. If you recognize your power, you are less likely to abuse it.

OBTAINING A MANDATE

Negotiators who look for a "fair deal", a "good deal", or the "best deal" do not have any specific goals. They do not want to commit themselves to specific goals because they are insecure. Maybe their goals could be wrong. Maybe they could get more. They hope for the best and usually achieve the worst. Instead of being pro-active in the pursuit of their goals, they are reactive to the other party.

As a negotiator you must have an end in mind. Negotiating is not a game. Without setting attainable goals, you cannot bargain effectively. If you establish attainable bargaining goals, you can plan how to structure the bargaining to achieve those goals. After giving your principal your advice, you will receive your marching orders, your instructions. These represent your principal's bargaining goals. You must insist that these goals be specific ones, although expressed wherever possible as a range. For example, *between* 4.5 and 5%. You cannot proceed with generalized goals.

In some cases, despite your advice, your principal's goals will not be realistic. So long as you have warned your principal, you will be able to go back for a changed mandate. This may also be necessary because of a change in the collective bargaining facts between the time of your original advice and the conclusion of negotiations. For example, a major settlement occurs in a comparable sector. Government funding levels change. Inflation takes off. The list is endless. You must keep current on developments as part of your on-going obligation to provide competent advice.

In some cases, negotiators actually prefer a limited mandate, knowing that ultimately their principal will move to a reasonable position. The reasons can vary, and depend on the circumstances. Thus, in many public sector disputes it is impossible to keep your mandate secret. If the other side knows your "bottom line" at the outset, it will be difficult for you to bargain effectively. No tactic or strategy will work. Your "throw-aways" will be transparent. On the other hand, with a limited mandate, the other team is left guessing. They are pretty sure your mandate will change, but they do not know when it will change, or what the change will be.

Again, with a limited mandate, you are able honestly to tell the other negotiator that a particular demand is beyond your mandate. "It is not my fault," you say, "but I cannot help you with that one." You are blaming your principal for rejecting a proposal, but your relationship with the other negotiator remains intact. As well, if you preface a position with the statement that you have gone as far as your mandate allows, there is less chance of raising a false expectation that you are flexible in the area under discussion. The more you talk about something, the more likely it is that it will become important. If the other side's demand cannot be achieved, say so at once. Do not lead anyone on.

You can expect that the other side will at some point request that you seek further instructions and obtain an enlarged mandate. Do not refuse to try. The effort to do so will preserve your relationship with the other negotiator. You will be able to say, "I did my best, but I couldn't sell it". Or you will return to the table armed with new instructions. The danger, of course, is that your "mandate" will no longer have credibility. That it can be changed has been proved. Eventually, you will have to say "No" and stick to it.

Principals who insist on an unrealistic mandate may believe that they will get more or pay less through this tactic because the negotiator who accepts the mandate will try harder to persuade the other party. Essentially, these principals are attempting to control the bargaining. Nothing more will be given away until it is clear that the previous offer will not sell. In this situation, the negotiator is dispatched as a messenger, while the principal does the actual bargaining. Sending a negotiator to the table in this fashion, without a realistic mandate, can only serve to create tensions, frustrate bargaining, and provoke a confrontation. Ultimately, resentment will build between principal and negotiator. This is not a prescription for success.

3

Preparing for Bargaining

TAKING STOCK

Your preparation for bargaining commences when you are first consulted. At that stage you will review the history of bargaining and research, in a preliminary way, the relevant collective bargaining facts. You will attempt to ascertain what your principals' goals are and how realistic (that is, achievable) you consider them to be.

If you are negotiating in a sector where compulsory arbitration prevails, you will have to factor into your opinion the prospects at arbitration. If strike/lockout is the régime, you will consider the consequences for your principals if a strike or lockout should take place.

The range of subject matter about which you can negotiate is, of course, unlimited. You must either research the subject matter yourself or have the research done by others. Your research should disclose all the data and arguments in support of your demands and all the data and arguments which do not support your demands. There is no point in playing ostrich. You may be able to distinguish an unfavourable fact. At the very least you will not be caught by surprise. Indeed, you will be able to structure your demands more effectively if you know which are strong, and which are weak.

COSTING THE CONTRACT

Because most bargaining is about money or money-related items (benefits), it is very important that you accurately "cost" the value of the existing collective agreement and the value of the changes which are proposed. I am often amazed as a mediator and arbitrator that the parties are unable to tell me what the cost is. One advantage of knowing the cost is that your principals can decide their priorities more realistically. Sometimes, objections to benefit changes fall away if it is determined that the cost is insignificant. I recall a dispute in which the employees wanted a large wage increase and a change in pensions. After I insisted that the costs be ascertained, it turned out that the pension change saved the employer more than enough money to fund the wage demand. I do not promise you this remarkable result every time you "cost", but when you know what you are talking about, your chances of succeeding are better. In the case of money, knowing what you are talking about means knowing what it costs.

TOTAL COMPENSATION

The breakdown of monetary demands into benefits and wage increases should not cause you to lose sight of the fact that you are still talking about money, about "total compensation". Indeed, it is universally accepted that bargaining should be on a "total compensation" basis. Total compensation is important in determining the appropriate level of wages and benefits of employees, relative to the wages of comparable employees, or the rate of inflation. Too often, the parties can't distinguish between cash and principle. The concept of "total compensation" will help to clear up the confusion. Yet, although I have heard the significance of total compensation preached since the day I began work as a mediator, it is poorly understood by many and not handled very well.

In a recent dispute, which centred on a demand by the employer to remove a retirement gratuity from a firefighters' contract, I made the following comments on "total compensation" in my capacity as an arbitrator:

> "The principal issue in dispute during this round of bargaining is the 'sick-leave retirement gratuity plan' which the employer seeks to grandfather [preserve for existing employees only]. The same issue has plagued the parties through several prior interest arbitrations and seems to be the stimulus for annual trips to the arbitral trough.
>
> In my respectful opinion, 'a sick-leave retirement gratuity plan' [pay-out of accumulated sick leave credits upon retirement] raises no issue of principle and should not prove any obstacle to bargaining. I will try to elaborate.
>
> On other occasions I have detailed the history in Ontario of the 'retirement gratuity' and the reasons which, in my opinion, make it an unsatisfactory way to provide insurance against

short-term illness. I will not repeat what I have said in the past. No argument has been advanced that would change this opinion.

However, I have concluded that this opinion, which I expressed 15 years ago in a case in which the battle lines were drawn on the basis of 'retirement gratuity—good or bad', is not helpful in resolving this or any other similar dispute. In fact, I now realize that it sets an arbitrator on the wrong course.

The principal problem with the 'retirement gratuity—good or bad' approach is that it converts what is really an issue of money into an issue of principle. The retirement gratuity represents a monetary cost to the employer which is part of the total compensation package for which employees bargain. Total compensation, of course, means the cost to the employer of both the salary and the benefits which employees earn. The division between salary and benefits is largely irrelevant to the employer. Equally, the makeup of the benefit package is a matter on the whole for the union to decide. These words of limitation recognize that there may be cases where the total compensation package as divided between salary and benefits, or the makeup of the benefit package, causes some problem for the employer in the retention or recruiting of employees. In those circumstances, of course, an employer can legitimately raise objection. No such problem exists in this case."

I concluded:

"The only relevant issue is whether the total compensation paid to these firefighters is reasonable vis-à-vis comparable firefighters and police. Unfortunately, in most cases the parties do not know what the total compensation cost is, notwithstanding that, for the past 15 years at least, interest arbitrators have been urged by the parties to have regard to total compensation. I have always endorsed the total compensation approach. It is a useful one because it requires the parties to take into account trade-offs in bargaining which involve allocation of funds to a benefit as opposed to salary. The accounts of the parties should be kept in dollars, not partly in dollars and partly in uncosted benefits ...

One may wonder how the debate as to the retirement gratuity evolved if the answer is as simple as I have suggested. Because the retirement gratuity is not expressed in dollar terms it has been treated erroneously as a non-monetary item. In the case of non-monetary items, a party who desires the introduction or deletion of such an item in a contract must satisfy two tests: rationality and process. By rationality I mean does the demand make sense? Is it a reasonable demand? Does it address a real problem? Does it abridge as little as possible the rights of the other party? By process, I mean can the demand be accommodated in the collective bargaining between the parties at this time given the other demands that also have to be addressed?

These tests are sensible ones for non-monetary items which may affect the workplace: management rights, productivity, safety, are examples. But the first test has no application to monetary demands. The justification for a money demand is determined by a consideration of comparability with employees in the same sector, if one is concerned about the level of income that a person ought to earn for the work performed, or with employees in the community, if one is addressing an issue of what is a normative wage increase for the particular year."

When you know the cost of each item, you can quickly calculate the value of the other team's offer or counter-offer. You can assess their latest move and better judge your own reaction. You can also give your principal accurate information about the real state of the bargaining.

You must also consider the "cost" of non-monetary items. How will a language change help you? Will it hurt the other side? Do you really need it? Are you trying to solve a problem which has arisen or avoid a "maybe" future problem? What is the other team's reaction likely to be? Will it worry and upset them? You must consider these and other relevant factors.

COSTING OTHER SETTLEMENTS

An important part of your preparation requires "costing" other settlements which you intend to use in support of your position or which the other side may advance against you. Without an accurate "costing", the relevance of these settlements is minimal.

Costing other agreements poses major problems. Many agreements are inaccurately reported, often deliberately so. For example, split increases of 2% effective January 1, 1992 and 2% effective July 1, 1992 may be reported as a 3% settlement, although this is only the cash-flow value of the settlement. Reporting the settlement at 4% ignores the fact that this is only the end rate. Is a reported increase of 5% the average increase for all employees in the bargaining unit? Or is it the increase for the entry level positions only? Or is it an across-the-board increase? Have additional steps been added to the wage grid so that certain wage increases are not included in the reported settlement at all? Have upward classification adjustments been bargained that do not count as wage increases? These are all matters which must be probed before a true costing can be made.

What is the value of agreed upon benefits? Of a merit increment? Of job security improvements? Of extra vacations when no additional personnel are hired to fill temporary vacancies, or when the increased vacation entitlement is contingent on completing years of service which no one will achieve during the term of the contract?

Benefits can range from 15-35% of total compensation. Thus, if wages are increased by 5%, but benefits are not increased at all, the total compensation increase may be only 3.5%. Beware of wage increases that are not reported as a percentage of total compensation.

Costing other settlements accurately is difficult because it is hard to obtain information from the parties or from data filed with the government. Even with full information, costing is an art that involves methods which are frequently controversial. Make sure you understand it, or that you consult someone who does.

STRUCTURING THE PACKAGE

You are now in a position to prepare your "package of demands" for bargaining. Structuring your package is very important. You must develop a package which allows you to end up with your bargaining goals. You will be including items whose purpose is to provide a supply of "trade-offs". These trade-offs are the "grease" which allows the bargaining to progress.

In developing your package you will also keep in mind how many "moves" you anticipate will be necessary before you achieve your goals. This factor depends on your own personal approach to bargaining and on the other side's approach. Consider this example. Your goal is 3%. If you believe that three moves will be necessary, you might start at 6% if you are the union, anticipating a move down to 4.5%, then 3.75%, then 3%. If you are the employer, and your goal is 3%, and you anticipate three moves, you would likely start at 1.5%, anticipating a move to 2.5%, then 3%. However, you should inform your principal of the "moves" you anticipate making as you proceed toward your goals. Otherwise, your principal will continually complain that you are giving things away and getting nothing in return.

It is important that you take pains to ensure that your principal fully understands the difference between your bargaining goals and your bargaining package. You do not want your bargaining package to be the standard against which your success or failure is measured. It is your bargaining goals against which success must be judged. Do not forget to keep your principal informed. So long as your bargaining goals are clearly defined, the bargaining steps will be judged in the light of your goals, and not on the basis that you are "giving up" your position.

DON'T FORGET YOUR TRADE-OFFS

Because your package will in fact include more than is necessary for a settlement, and the other party will know this, the skill in structuring is to make it difficult to assess what the trade-offs are. The more plausible your trade-offs, the more credible your bargaining position will appear. When you make concessions, the other party will feel that it has really accomplished some gains. If your trade-offs are frivolous, and command neither respect nor attention, your "core" demands will be more difficult to achieve.

You should appreciate that it is hard to camouflage trade-offs if they involve a monetary cost. You will likely be asked to cost all of your demands. The other party, if properly advised, will bargain a total compensation cost and let you distribute it between wages and benefits.

4

Needs,
Not Demands

UNDERSTAND YOUR NEEDS

In preparing your demands, it is important that you develop the reasons why you "need" the demand. What problem are you seeking to solve or to avoid? You will find the other side is more receptive to what you need than to what you merely want. Human nature is such that people ordinarily respond to the needs of others but resent their demands.

It is also vital that your demand correspond with your need. An inflated demand usually generates what I call an inflated denial. In other words, if you ask for more than you need, the other side will find it easy to say no because the real need is buried by the excessiveness of the demand. When I mediate, frequently I am able to settle an issue by asking the party making the demand to explain the need. When the demand is reduced to the point where it corresponds with the need, and no more, the objections of the other party often fall away. Rarely will a limited demand which corresponds to a real need harm the legitimate interest of the other party. Once a party agrees that it will not be harmed, it is difficult to refuse to co-operate. I find that any lingering resistance disappears when I repeat what my father once told me: "If it doesn't hurt you, why not do it?".

AN EXAMPLE

To illustrate this point, I use the following example. A wife comes home from work, tired and depressed; the day has been miserable. A night out with friends seems a perfect remedy. If a demand is made, "I want to go out tonight", the response will likely be a negative one. "Why? You went out last night, I am tired of staying home alone". This prompts the reply, "I have a right to go out". You can picture for yourself the balance of the conversation. If, on the other hand, the wife begins with an outline of the horrible day, how depressing it has been, how nice it would be to spend an evening with friends, a positive response is virtually guaranteed. Bargaining is no different.

Not all non-monetary demands relate to problems which have already arisen. Some demands are prophylactic, i.e. they are designed to avoid a problem in the future. Because the problem has not yet arisen, its boundaries are not clearly definable. In these circumstances, your demand should be sufficiently expansive to allow for the likelihood that bargaining will reduce its compass. With an actual need, based on an existing problem, your demand should be more closely tailored to the required solution.

5

Setting the Ground Rules

EXCHANGING BARGAINING PACKAGES

Some collective agreements require that the parties exchange their respective packages in advance. In other situations, an exchange is a matter of agreement as part of the "ground rules" of bargaining. Generally speaking, I consider this a poor practice. The party who wants changes should be required to submit its package. Otherwise, by requiring a simultaneous exchange, you will stimulate the development of issues for bargaining which may not be serious or real. Moreover, once proffered, these will not be readily abandoned. It would be preferable to allow the other party to examine your demands before submitting its response. Although this response may also include a "shopping list", it is not likely to be as long as it would be if produced in advance of your position.

WHERE AND WHEN TO BARGAIN

The best place is one in which you feel comfortable. The worst place is one in which you feel uncomfortable. It is not reasonable to expect the employer to bargain at the union hall. Equally, it is unreasonable to expect the union to bargain in the employer's executive offices. A neutral place, such as a hotel, is preferable. When I mediate, I always insist on a neutral locale. Insistence on bargaining in your premises will only create an unnecessary issue, and may serve to stir up resentment and stiffen the resolve to resist your demands.

Apart from an initial brief session to exchange opening positions, bargaining should be conducted during ordinary working hours. The practice of bargaining after work is unsatisfactory. By that time, people are tired and short-tempered. It is impossible to build any momentum. Only when a settlement is in sight should you engage in all-night bargaining.

HOW OFTEN TO BARGAIN

Bargaining will be more effective if the parties have a time limit. If you bargain only after work, it will take forever. If you bargain during the day, it should not take more than a few days. Start on a Monday morning and agree that, if you have not settled by Thursday morning, that's it. It should rarely be necessary to request an adjournment to obtain instructions or a new mandate. The negotiator should have a reasonable mandate before the bargaining starts. You ought not to make a career out of negotiating a contract.

On the other hand, if you know that your mandate is not reasonable, do not schedule three or four days of bargaining. Schedule only one day, in anticipation of having to seek new instructions. Nothing frustrates momentum in bargaining like delay, particularly delay which involves people sitting around and doing nothing. And stopping early only adds to the sense of failure.

6

Organizing
the Bargaining

PACKAGE OR ISSUE-BY-ISSUE BARGAINING

The practice of many negotiators is to package bargain. They submit an offer on all items and attempt to negotiate the whole package at one time. This approach is rarely successful because the other party will accept the best items in the package and respond with a series of additional demands. You will be forced to withdraw some of the items that had previously been offered in order to counter some of the other side's additional demands. Pretty soon you are bargaining backwards. In my opinion, package bargaining should be avoided.

A preferable approach, although it doesn't work all that well either, is to proceed on an issue-by-issue basis. The parties usually commence with non-monetary or "language items", and try to sign these off as the bargaining proceeds. "Signing off" means reaching a final agreement on the point regardless how the rest of the issues are resolved. The problem with this approach is that many negotiators are afraid to agree to something because of fear that the entire bargain will not be satisfactory. Moreover, if items are signed off, there will be fewer opportunities for trade-off in the event that the dispute goes to mediation; this makes it harder for the mediator because there is less to work with.

THE PREFERRED APPROACH

The best approach is to state, right at the outset, that there is no deal on anything unless there is a deal on everything. In other words, agreements on specific items are tentative only, and can be withdrawn if the total package is not acceptable. This encourages the parties to settle less important matters without the fear of ending up with an unsatisfactory package. One might argue that there is little value in clearing away minor items if an overall deal is not concluded. But the process of resolving minor items engenders confidence and trust, and builds momentum in settling the monetary issues which are usually left to the end. I have seldom seen a settlement founder over non-monetary issues. You may be met with the objection: "You are asking me to agree to something that you want. But what about the items that we want?". The correct response is: "What have you got to worry about? If you don't like the whole deal, you don't have to take it."

I recommend that, in the absence of a third party neutral, you enter into a written agreement setting out the ground rules, because human nature is such that tentative settlements are felt emotionally to be final settlements. You do not want to create unrealistic expectations. Of course, there is nothing to prevent the parties from deciding to sign off tentatively agreed items, even if a complete settlement proves unattainable. What is important is that you make a conscious choice as to the approach you take, and communicate it to the other side, so that there are no misunderstandings.

SETTING THE BARGAINING AGENDA

As I have noted, the theory of settling the money last is based on the notion that resolving language issues will build confidence, trust and momentum. The parties invest their time and energy, and become committed to a deal. This makes them more flexible when they deal with the sole remaining issue of money. Unions prefer this approach, too, because it is rare that non-monetary items are strike issues, and if the money is settled first, there is little incentive for the employer to settle anything else. If the union is going to go on strike, it prefers to do so over money, though it may still be intent on achieving other outstanding language demands.

Ordinarily, I follow this course as a mediator because it would be seen as too radical if I did not. However, in some respects, I question its common sense. Arguing about minor items can engender a lot of ill feelings, and resolution of them is not likely to persuade anybody on the money. Indeed, the opposite is true. If you can reach agreement on the money, the other issues usually fall into place or by the wayside, simply because they are rarely "strike issues", i.e. issues worth taking or going to strike over.

Thus, on a few occasions, I have mediated the money first. For one thing, money is not always the most contentious issue in dispute. There are some cases where the parties are very close on the money issue. Pattern-setting agreements may have been reached for comparable groups of employees, and these may narrow the "zone of settlement", especially where the parties have a history of following them. In these circumstances, negotiators are likely to focus their attention on benefits and working conditions. On the other hand, as I have said, if the money is settled, it takes a lot of the steam out of everything else.

In one negotiation, when I was told by the parties that they were miles apart on the money and that a settlement was impossible, I put it first on the bargaining agenda. Why waste time on everything else, I asked, if the money could not be solved? When I proceeded to mediate the negotiations over money, I was able to see that, instead of being miles apart, the parties were actually only inches apart. But I do not consider a mediation successful unless everything is settled. In my view, "settling everything but" is no settlement at all. I decided that there was no need to settle the money to the last penny, and I moved on to the other items, knowing that at the appropriate moment, once the other items were resolved, I could put the whole deal together.

The point I am making is that there is no hard and fast rule about the order of bargaining. Try to develop an order which will lead to a settlement most efficiently. If the other team insists on a particular order, exercise caution because they may present as the first item something they desperately want; if you agree on this item, you may find them disinclined to compromise on any others.

USING SUBCOMMITTEES

It sometimes proves useful, especially in complex disputes, to separate out some of the issues and assign them to sub-committees to discuss, to draft and to present proposals to the main bargaining committee. It is important in this kind of bargaining, which may continue for a number of days, that everybody keep working. If all members of the bargaining team are contributing, the bargaining will be more effective. In my experience, members of a bargaining team with nothing to do are often tempted to exercise power in a negative way. If they contribute to the bargaining, they will want to see their contribution bear fruit; in effect they become emotionally committed to a settlement. Bargaining is no different from any other form of interaction between human beings. Making everyone feel important is vital. You must, of course, ensure that the individuals assigned to subcommittees are fully briefed on the items in issue.

7

Moving the Negotiations Along

SET SENSIBLE GOALS

If you know where you are going you can get there quickly. Having reasonable bargaining goals and a sensible "package" should permit you to proceed expeditiously. Obviously, if the other party does not know where it is going or, what is worse, how to get there, progress will be difficult. Let me offer you a few suggestions.

If the other team is confident that a "deal" will be achieved, they will be more forthcoming and co-operative. If you start off with a ridiculous opening package, you will shake that confidence. You will weaken it further by taking forever to respond to proposals. An insistence that the other side reduce the number of its demands before you respond is, again, very unhelpful. Getting caught in untruths or providing inaccurate, misleading or incomplete data also hurts progress. Avoid all of the above.

BUILDING MOMENTUM

When the other team responds, prepare your own response quickly. If their response is positive, make your response positive. If they are going a bit slowly, you can go more slowly as long as you continue forwards and not backwards. If you delay in responding for hours on end, you create the impression that you do not know what you are doing.

You must not be impatient. These negotiations are important. You want to be careful. Do not throw caution to the wind. But there is no reason for complete inertia. If the other side cannot respond, adjourn to the next day. There is nothing more frustrating for your team than to wait around for hours and then adjourn without a proposal.

As proposals are exchanged, meet with the other negotiator privately. Try to plan future moves. Get a sense of whether the other team is "on side" in wanting to conclude a settlement. This is particularly the case on minor issues, for it can save a lot of time if you reach consensus on what can be achieved. If you believe the other side is moving too slowly, let your opposite number know. They may not realize it.

MOVING TO MEDIATION

The only way to effect a settlement without resort to a neutral is for the negotiators to develop a good working relationship and sufficient trust in each other that they can determine whether a deal is possible. If a deal is not in the cards, it is better to end the bargaining quickly than to irritate everyone with fruitless bargaining sessions. If the bargaining is merely a ritual until a mediator arrives, there is no point in wasting any time. Meet, say hello, and bid goodbye. Even where bargaining does take place, the parties will often be reluctant to expose their actual bottom lines because they want to save something in the event of mediation. As a neutral I expect this. If you do not keep something in reserve, how can I get the matter settled?

8

Developing Confidence and Trust

MEETING WITH
THE OTHER NEGOTIATOR

It is essential that you persuade the other team that they can have confidence in your ability to negotiate effectively and that you can be trusted not to cheat, betray, unpleasantly surprise or otherwise disappoint them. In this regard, it is often helpful to meet the other negotiator with no one else present before the actual negotiations begin. You can let your counterpart know where you are going, in general terms. The other negotiator is likely to reciprocate by giving you an opinion of the likely chances of success and an indication of the other side's primary areas of interest. These discussions will help you to avoid surprises, plan strategy and appear to be in command. Your principal will feel secure.

As the negotiations proceed, these meetings will continue to be useful. The other team may be moving too slowly but may not be aware of it. Messages to this effect can be exchanged at such meetings. In addition, you can forewarn the other negotiator of any moves you may make which might otherwise prove surprising or embarrassing. Meetings of this kind engender trust and confidence. Take advantage of them.

THE ART OF GRATUITOUS GIVING

Years ago, Stanley Hartt, then a prominent Montreal lawyer, arbitrator and mediator, told me the biblical story of the burning bush, and how it persuaded the Israelites that Moses was a true prophet. Mediators, Hartt claimed, need to produce their own magical "burning bush" to persuade the parties that they are true mediators. This lesson applies equally to negotiators even when mediators are not present.

I define a "burning bush" as obtaining agreement on a contentious issue quickly which until that point had proved intractable, or achieving a significant modification of the way in which the parties relate to each other. Let me illustrate.

When I act as a mediator, the first thing that I do after my appointment is to ascertain the issues in dispute. One sometimes discovers that perceptions vary about what is in dispute and the relative importance of what is in dispute. In the first instance, I meet separately with each of the parties. What I usually discover at these sessions is that there are issues which each party is willing to surrender but which excite anxiety in the other party. Presto! I have discovered the "burning bush". After establishing the agenda for bargaining, I settle these very simple issues and immediately acquire the confidence and trust of the parties. I am a true mediator!

As a negotiator, you can do the same thing. By making a small concession, or by withdrawing a relatively insignificant demand, without asking anything in return, the other side will appreciate what you have done and will develop an attitude which is more compromising and more suited to settlement.

Indeed, it becomes extremely difficult for the other party not to respond in a positive way. You have produced a "burning bush", and you are immediately identified as a reasonable person who is accommodating, even in an adversarial atmosphere.

If you have worked with the other negotiator before and have been successful in achieving a settlement, the "burning bush" is less important. Confidence and trust already exist. In new situations, however, it is essential to develop confidence and trust as soon as possible.

NEVER EMBARRASS THE OTHER PARTY

If negotiating were a game, embarrassing the other party would probably be worth some points. But it is not a game. Success is not measured by your cleverness, aggressiveness or tactical smarts. It is measured by whether or not you succeed in reaching a fair settlement. Embarrassing the other negotiator will impair and even destroy your ability to settle.

There are numerous ways of embarrassing the other negotiator. Some involve little more than acts of discourtesy or disrespect. Others, of greater significance, entail exploitation of an error made by the other party. This frequently occurs in drafting. A clause drafted by the other negotiator may inaccurately reflect the parties' intent in a way which favours your principal. Sooner or later the error will be discovered. Don't wait. Point it out yourself. Your duty to your principal does not involve your taking advantage of such a mistake. Again, to avoid embarrassment, forewarn the other negotiator of any dramatic actions or changes in your bargaining position.

Here is another example which arises frequently. You have made a counter-offer. The response shows little or no movement from the other side's original position. Some negotiators will refuse to make a further offer until the other party improves its position. What you are doing is forcing the other party to bargain against itself. Although this may appear justifiable, it will humiliate and embarrass the other negotiator. A better approach is to express disappointment at the other side's position and the snail-like pace of the bargaining. Nevertheless, make another offer with some movement and combine it with a warning that you expect more movement or the negotiations are going to fall apart.

DISCUSS FULLY, DRAFT FAIRLY

Some negotiators try to win their points by clever drafting. This tactic not only annoys the other side; it destroys trust. Discuss your problems directly and fully. Then, having settled the issue in principle, draft language which reflects the settlement. Do not try through drafting to "improve" the deal. An improvement of this kind is known as a "kicker", probably because the arrival of an unexpected additional demand feels like a kick in the stomach.

9

Communicating Effectively

RECOGNIZING BODY LANGUAGE

Throughout this book I have emphasized the importance of recognizing the emotional reactions of your principal, yourself and the other party. Only if you understand these reactions can you attempt to defuse them. This talent is probably the single most important skill that the successful negotiator must develop. Understanding emotional reactions goes hand in hand with recognizing non-verbal communications, so-called "body language".

You must learn to listen carefully and to observe closely. Most of us are preoccupied with our own babble, the priceless music of our own voice. You can learn more from listening to how others speak and by watching their gestures. You can often distinguish real confidence from mere bravado. You can tell genuine interest from pretended concern. You can separate the true notes from those that are false. But you must listen attentively, calmly and receptively, ready to discern the slightest message, and you must keep a close eye on non-verbal, body language. Communication is not limited to words. What should you be looking for?

- a stutter from an otherwise glib speaker
- a bobbing of the Adam's apple
- a nervous tic, a cheek twitching
- eyes which suddenly do not meet yours
- an unexpected lowering of the voice
- hands which cannot be still
- papers being rustled, fidgeting.

The list is endless. You have only to watch and listen. You have to become a communications detective. Then, you must develop the confidence to rely on the signals you detect.

UNDERSTANDING YOURSELF

Even then, all of this may not be enough. You will learn little about *yourself*. How *you* communicate. Whether people believe *you*. Do they trust *you*? Do they like *you*? Some negotiators believe that analysis or group therapy helps you to understand yourself, and improve your effectiveness in bargaining. You can learn about yourself through observing your own behaviour in others. You can spot hidden agendas, recognize attempts at rationalizing conduct, get in touch with your own feelings. You can learn more about negotiating in group therapy than from any seminar, conference or book devoted to teaching negotiating skills. Indeed, it is hard to question the value of a knowledge of human nature, and the advantages to be gained from modern techniques of clinical psychology.

KEEP THE LINES OPEN

Unless you are able to communicate effectively and ensure that the lines of communication remain open, your negotiations will not likely succeed. However, in many disputes the parties are unable to discuss issues in a constructive way, because of hostility between opposing negotiators. The dislike may be so intense that one side stops listening altogether to the other. The danger is that the parties, in closing their ears to the insults and jibes, may fail to hear any positive signals that may emerge.

My remedy for this problem, in one case, was to convene a meeting of the parties. I asked the union spokesperson to explain why the union's demands were warranted. I then asked the employer's spokesperson to reply. We proceeded issue by issue. Personal attacks immediately ceased. Shouting and screaming or other unseemly behaviour was not permitted. This worked very well. The parties found they could talk to each other in a civilized fashion. In a little while I ordered coffee and refreshments for everyone. We had a break. The parties mingled and chatted. If you discuss the news of the day over coffee pleasantly, it is hard to be unpleasant over other issues.

As negotiators, you should take care to avoid a breakdown in communications because of animosities between members of the opposing bargaining teams. You will find it easier to negotiate if the individuals involved get along and relate to each other like human beings.

THE VIRTUES OF VENTILATION

In negotiations, it is sometimes necessary to allow the other team to ventilate their feelings. I'll tell you how I first discovered this important fact. In the first year or so of my work as a mediator I was asked to assist in resolving a school board-teacher dispute. The parties had reached a tentative settlement, but the teachers had failed to ratify. Although I had mediated a number of disputes, I had never before had to deal with the aftermath of a non-ratification vote.

I began the mediation by meeting with the school board trustees but could make no progress at all. No matter how hard I tried, I couldn't get to first base. None of my arguments worked. I left completely dejected and perplexed. During the three-hour drive home I tried to analyze what had occurred. The only thing the trustees had wanted to talk about was the non-ratification and its impact on them. I had not wanted to discuss the non-ratification at all because it was history. I was determined to get on with settling the matter.

The more I thought about it, the more I realized how angry the trustees were over the non-ratification. They felt that they had put their best foot forward and it had not achieved the settlement they thought it would. What would they now have to give to get an agreement? How could they trust the other negotiators? Could I guarantee them a deal? They felt that they were made to look stupid. They were very resentful. Gradually it dawned on me that, until these hostile feelings were resolved, no resolution of the remaining issues in dispute would be possible.

What to do? The first thing I did when I returned to the mediation was to encourage the trustees to express their feelings about the non-ratification. I let everyone speak who wanted to do so. I then acknowledged the validity of their reaction and I sympathized with their predicament. I expressed the hope that, notwithstanding this unfortunate event, we would be able, in a positive way, to resolve the matter. I then left to meet with the teachers.

When I returned to the trustees' room their attitude had completely changed. They were ready to get on with a solution. The dispute was quickly settled. And why? Because they had been allowed an opportunity to ventilate.

10

Telling
the Truth

THE BENEFITS OF CANDOUR

"Always tell the truth. No one will believe you anyway." My father, who gave me this advice, confined his remarks to money, but I think the idea has wider application, especially in the area of negotiation. No one expects you to tell the truth when you negotiate. Therefore, you have nothing to lose by doing so.

As a mediator I often encounter the attitude, implied if not expressed, that I must be lying to the parties because mediators never tell the truth. The feeling is that mediators manipulate through deceit. I always respond by repeating my father's aphorism.

In fact, when I mediate, I never lie. Apart from moral considerations, there are a number of good reasons for not lying in negotiations. If you do not tell both parties the same story, they are likely to discover it. You cannot depend on confidentiality. In my experience, there is always someone on each bargaining team who is talking to someone on the other bargaining team. A mediator who is found to be a liar loses credibility and trust.

Successful negotiations depend on mutual trust. This can be irretrievably destroyed by lies or deceit. Therefore, I recommend that you do not lie. This rule against lying applies not only to your relationship with the other party but to your relationship with your own principal. I think we underestimate the ability of people to accept the truth. We hide it from them because we fear their reaction. My experience is that people are a lot smarter than we generally give them credit for being. We can safely tell them the truth.

There is little skill in telling lies. If the truth is not acceptable, so be it. When I first started to mediate, I observed a very skillful management lawyer carefully explain some complex management proposals to the union's bargaining committee. He pointed out all of the consequences, both positive and negative. He did not shrink from the negative. He told the truth. I was quite surprised by his candour. After all, the prevailing rule of conduct among lawyers in real estate negotiations is *caveat emptor:* let the buyer beware! Only if a specific question is asked is a truthful answer required. I remember thinking that this lawyer is going to wreck the negotiations with so much honesty. In fact, his candour was appreciated by the union's bargaining committee, and the matter was settled. I have never forgotten this lesson. In an on-going relationship, that is, one where the parties continue to interact after the settlement, people will get even if you have tricked them. Your settlement will buy only a temporary peace.

POSTURING IS PERMITTED

I do not want to mislead you about "telling the truth". Obviously, in a sense, asking for 10% when you really will settle for 7%, is not strictly truthful. But there is no requirement that demands accurately reflect your bottom line and there is no expectation of this. In fact, expectations are to the contrary. Bargaining would grind to a halt if all negotiators told the "truth" in this sense.

Is it lying to raise the prospect of a strike or lockout, or a breakdown in negotiations if that prospect has little reality? Again, in a sense, it is a pretence, but it is not objectionable. These kinds of suggestions are part of the give-and-take of bargaining. Again, in a literal sense, tactics such as feigning surprise or ignorance may involve bluff. But, here too, no one is relying on you to tell the truth. What you must not lie about are facts: the cost of benefits; settlements reached with comparable groups; bargaining history; plans for workforce adjustment. These must be fully and honestly disclosed. You cannot mislead the other party by providing incomplete or deceptive information, or by withholding crucial information.

ALWAYS, ALWAYS DELIVER

You must not make undertakings that you are unable to honour. If you promise to provide the other side with information or details of your position, a failure to honour your undertaking will destroy your credibility and undermine the confidence that the other party has in you. As I have said before, mutual trust must be fostered if negotiations are to succeed. Never threaten what you are not prepared to do. You will never be believed again if your bluff is called and you do not follow through. It is one thing to refer to a strike as a possibility. It is quite another thing to promise or threaten that there will be one unless you intend to carry out your threat.

When you tell the other side that your principal will agree to something, you must be able to deliver on your promises. That is the mark of a professional negotiator. In this context I am referring not only to promises which are explicitly made but to the signals which you give to the other side about the positions that you anticipate taking as the give-and-take of bargaining proceeds. If you mislead, even inadvertently, by giving signals that you subsequently disavow, you will completely destroy your own reputation, as well as any basis for mutual trust. If you want to be successful, you have to be a person whom others can depend on.

The most damaging example of a failure to deliver is a tentative settlement followed by a failure to secure ratification. There is nothing more destructive to the bargaining relationship than this result. More about this later.

11

Using Leverage

USING LEVERAGE WISELY

The recognition and/or creation of leverage in negotiations is an important subject. By "leverage" I mean a circumstance which puts you at an advantage or the other party at a disadvantage in the negotiations or vice versa. Sometimes leverage can be created. At other times leverage exists without your doing anything to create it. You have only to recognize it and to take advantage of the opportunity.

In bargaining over wages, for example, leverage arises when the employer "needs" the employees. Business is booming, orders are backlogged, and the competition is knocking on the door. Conversely, in more difficult economic times when layoffs are a threat, the employer can insist on a more favourable bargain and may even be able to "claw back" prior concessions or achievements.

As a general rule, you should exercise prudence in an ongoing relationship in taking too much advantage of leverage opportunities. Memories are long. "Getting even" can disrupt a relationship. My father used to quote an expression that captures this point: "Be careful when you dig a hole for someone else lest you fall into it".

EXPLOITING CHANGES IN LEVERAGE

You may be confronted with a situation where the other team has shown little interest in negotiating. Suddenly, they are knocking down your door, pressing for a settlement. Chances are that the locus of leverage has changed. You may not know what the change is but you can be reasonably confident that a change has occurred. In labour-management negotiations, leverage may shift if business conditions change, or some other settlements are about to be reached which will significantly affect your dispute, or the government gets ready to announce higher or lower funding levels.

Regard with suspicion any sudden unexpected change in bargaining attitude. It will usually signal a change in leverage. On the other hand, if you want to modify your own bargaining position due to changing circumstances which have altered the leverage, try if you can to develop a scenario that will allay suspicion. You might even consider coming clean in the expectation that it is more difficult for the other team to justify to themselves taking advantage of your candour than it would be to take advantage of your predicament if you withheld it and they discovered it themselves.

THE USE OF THREATS

It is considered acceptable to threaten or institute civil proceedings, such as a lawsuit, even where the purpose is to create leverage in bargaining. Assume that a *bona fide* dispute arises between a vendor and purchaser of real estate as to whether an agreement has in fact been reached. In order to prevent the vendor from selling to another party, the purchaser proceeds to institute a lawsuit, thereby "tying up" the land until the court rules on the merits of the claim. Should this occur, the vendor may be "levered" into settling, in the interest of immediate disposition of the property. Litigation provides a prime opportunity to create leverage for settlement.

Let us assume that you know that the other party has committed a crime. Can you threaten to report the crime to the authorities in order to obtain a settlement? Clearly not, for in these circumstances you would be guilty of extortion. Section 346 of the *Canadian Criminal Code* provides as follows:

> 346.(1) Every one commits extortion who, without reasonable justification or excuse and with intent to obtain anything, by threats, accusations, menaces or violence induces or attempts to induce any person, whether or not he is the person threatened, accused or menaced or to whom violence is shown, to do anything or cause anything to be done.
>
> (1.1) Every one who commits extortion is guilty of an indictable offence and liable to a maximum term of imprisonment for life.
>
> (2) A threat to institute civil proceedings is not a threat for the purposes of this section.

Can you threaten to report people to the income tax authorities or to a professional disciplinary body if they refuse to settle? I recommend against use of these threats as well. In my opinion, here too, you may be guilty of extortion.

CREATING LEVERAGE

You can create leverage by the way in which you organize your bargaining. In Canada, bargaining is decentralized, and takes place on a plant-by-plant basis between the union and the employer. But there are many exceptions. The construction industry in some jurisdictions bargains on a province-wide basis for each major trade group. Federal government employees bargain on a national basis. Central bargaining, where the right to strike exists, can be seen as creating leverage in favour of the union. A strike will be province-wide instead of being merely local. The result will often be standardized pay scales and system-wide benefits. A merger of bargaining units, as occurred at Canada Post, will also strengthen the union's hand in bargaining because a strike will be that much more effective in curtailing service.

On the other hand, centralized bargaining reduces the opportunities to "divide and conquer", or to "whipsaw" and "leapfrog". "Whipsawing" entails achieving a settlement with one employer and using it to persuade another employer to agree to a similar settlement. Consider this example. The police in Oakville may historically compare themselves with the police in Burlington and Hamilton. If the police co-ordinate their bargaining, they can choose the municipality with which they have the best relationship and try to settle there first. They can then "whipsaw" the other municipalities with this settlement. The same approach is used by teachers with school boards, and by the autoworkers' union with the Big Three.

"Leapfrogging" is a variation of "whipsawing". The only difference is that the union seeks to achieve a higher settlement than the one it has made with a comparable employer on the basis that the employees of the latter have historically earned less. When the employees of the comparable employer have received "catch-up" to compensate for falling behind other groups or the rate of inflation, a "ripple effect" can result.

This is not to say that employers don't also play the "whipsaw" game, by co-ordinating their bargaining and settling early with the union that offers the cheapest deal. Indeed, the employers' perspective is but a mirror image of the unions'. Centralized or co-ordinated bargaining allows them to avoid the whipsaw effect. On the other hand, it results in greater bargaining leverage for the union, and for this reason some employers seek to break up broader-based bargaining.

Much of what you observe on the labour relations scene is the jockeying that goes on as the parties seek to create greater leverage for themselves.

12

Tactics to Watch Out For

THE LIMITATIONS OF TACTICS

A knowledge of tactics is necessary, not so much to enable you to utilize them as to enable you to recognize and counteract their use by the other side. The fact is that many negotiators over-indulge in tactics in the mistaken belief that effective negotiations require them. In my opinion, you can negotiate quite effectively without any knowledge of tactics if you have a thorough knowledge of the subject-matter, obtain a sensible mandate from your principals, make an effective presentation of your demands, and have a reasonable attitude toward the goal of negotiation.

The tactics you will encounter most frequently are the "high ball" and the "low ball". I do not recommend these tactics, for they lead to confrontation. If you are faced with a party who utilizes them, simply press on to strike/lockout. Letting the other team know that these tactics will result only in confrontation is the best way to persuade them to become more reasonable. Let me explain why.

THE "HIGH BALL"

The "high ball" offer is one which is unrealistically high. You are asking for far too much. The advantage of this approach is that you create the impression of giving up a lot when you finally settle, and thereby enhance the other party's sense of accomplishment. It is important to note, however, that "high balling" is different from structuring an offer so as to leave yourself room to negotiate, by including trade-offs and/or setting your monetary demands at a point higher than your bottom line. This is not a "high ball" because it is not so far removed from the range of reasonable that you lose credibility.

The principal disadvantage of the "high ball" offer is that it gives the other side the impression that you do not seriously intend to settle. It provokes a "low ball" response or no response at all. The other party may say "we will talk when you get serious". Negotiations may stall. You may have to submit another offer. In the latter case, your loss of credibility will be significant. You will end up bargaining against yourself.

In addition, "high balling" prolongs negotiations. To create any credibility in your "high ball", you will have to stick with it for a long time. Only then will the other party feel compelled to take you seriously and begin to question its own assumption about what is a reasonable settlement. This form of intimidation takes a long time. It is a pointlessly self-destructive approach to "high ball" and then quickly lower your offer significantly. Not only do you lose credibility, but the other party will also think that there may be no end to your downward drift.

THE "LOW BALL"

The "low ball" offer involves the same approach looked at from the opposite perspective. It suffers the same disadvantages. Nevertheless, if you are prepared to tough it out, it can be effective. When I first started to practise, I encountered an experienced lawyer who specialized in the "low ball" technique. If the case was worth $25,000, he would offer $5,000. At the outset you would laugh at it and your client would laugh at it. But after months passed and nothing more was offered, your client would become edgy. Your client would think that after all this lawyer is a senior, experienced member of the bar and maybe he knows something we don't know. It is not easy to restrain a client who is subjected to a well thought out "low ball". Eventually, as the case approached trial, this lawyer would offer $10,000. By that stage, you would have to cut your client's hand off to stop him from grabbing it; it would look so good.

The "low ball" may be a more effective tactic than the "high ball" simply because the offer is made by the party who is going to pay. The "high ball" offer is made by the party who is seeking to obtain something. The influence of the "high ball" tactic on the mind of the party who controls the purse strings is probably never as great as the influence of the "low ball" tactic on the mind of the party who is seeking something.

THE FEINT

Another tactic, which I call the "feint", in reality involves a "high ball" or a "low ball" offer, but it is not readily recognizable, and can, therefore, be very effective. It works this way. You make a demand that you do not in fact want but which you know the other party cannot tolerate and then you ride it for all it is worth. Consider an example. Minimum staffing is a favourite demand with some unions; to the employer it is a provision to be resisted at all costs. If you were to include a minimum staffing requirement in your demands, even though you really did not want it, this would represent a "high ball", although not a detectable one. The employer may be willing to buy its way out of this demand by offering better terms on demands that you are serious about, and may regard such a result as a considerable victory. Conversely, an employer can "low ball" on the issue of minimum staffing by demanding its removal from the collective agreement if it already exists as a provision, even though the employer is not really serious about the issue. A judgement must be made about whether a party is serious or not when it includes such items in an offer or counter-offer.

TAKE IT OR LEAVE IT

Many negotiators dislike the nuts and bolts of bargaining as it is practised generally. They find the give-and-take and the apparent haggling over nickels and dimes disturbing. A tactic which avoids this process involves the presentation of a fixed position combined with a refusal to bargain over it with the other side's negotiating team. This take-it-or-leave-it approach is known as "Boulwarism" after its author, Lemuel Boulware of General Electric, who adopted this bargaining tactic. It was ultimately declared an unfair labour practice by the U.S. National Labor Relations Board.

This tactic humiliates the other team because it strips them of any meaningful role in the bargaining process, and it is not likely to lead to a settlement unless the offer is so generous as to be irresistible. Human nature is such that the other team will try for more and be unhappy if they do not achieve it. For no one will believe that a party would start by putting its bottom line on the table. This tactic is a no-no!

THE "BRER RABBIT" PLOY

You will recall that Brer Rabbit begged not to be thrown into the briar patch when in fact that was what he desperately wanted. Why? Brer Rabbit believed that human nature is such that people will refuse to do what is wanted and are anxious to do what is not wanted. However cynical this view, it probably reflects a shrewd appreciation of the subconscious behaviour of many people.

Using reverse psychology in the context of negotiations is probably a dangerous ploy, and best avoided. The only importance of the Brer Rabbit tactic is to alert you to your own visceral instinct to say "No" to everything the other team wants, and "Yes" to everything they do not want. Indeed, sensible solutions are often rejected for no other reason than that the opposite party proposed them. Hidden agendas are suspected where none in fact may exist. In collective bargaining, paranoia is an occupational hazard.

CONFESSION AND AVOIDANCE

Sometimes, the other side may accept your proposal, but attach conditions which make the proposal undesirable. This tactic is called "confession and avoidance", after the legal practice of admitting the other side's facts (confession), while disputing that those facts warrant relief (avoidance). By shifting the battleground in this way, the other party avoids a frontal denial of your proposal and preserves the appearance of acting reasonably.

Consider this example. The union wants to have a steward present whenever any discipline is to be imposed by the employer. The employer objects to the demand, but is hesitant to deny it outright, and instead adds a condition to acceptance of the union's proposal to the effect that the steward may be present but cannot speak. This condition is certain to result in rejection. This tactic skirts the border of good faith bargaining, and should be recognized for what it is.

TACTICS ARE OVER-RATED

The problem many negotiators have is that their approach to bargaining is like my approach to golf. I think new golf clubs or a different golf ball will make me a better golfer. These negotiators think that tactics pave the way to bargaining glory. The truth is that tactics are useful to further a bargaining goal, but no tactic is a substitute for preparing sensible bargaining goals.

13

Appealing
to Conscience

TAKING RESPONSIBILITY

In one case, in which I mediated a dispute involving a major public institution, it was reported to me that the head of the institution was taking an inflexible position in the expectation that the matter would go to arbitration. If the result was good, he would take credit for having employed the process; if the result was bad, he would blame the arbitrator. I decided to meet with this individual directly, in the presence of his negotiator. We had a long talk in which I frankly acknowledged that he could indeed proceed to arbitration, and that many people would take the easy way out, but that it was not good for the institution to have its affairs settled by a third party, because it destroyed collegiality, and would set an unhealthy precedent for the future. I said that I did not think that he was the type of person who would avoid taking responsibility in this way, and that I was sure that he would do the right thing. He did.

ASKING FOR HELP

Appealing to the other side for help is a bargaining tactic which can be used effectively. Let us assume that you want a dental plan with an orthodontic rider. Rather than making this a demand, you meet with the other party and explain that there are many children of employees with orthodontic problems. You ask for help in solving this problem. You pretend that you do not know what to do, that you are not aware that insurance is available. Ask for help. Helping other people makes us feel happy. People like to do what makes them feel happy. In the result, this approach can often be successful.

When I was a young lawyer, I employed this tactic in a negotiation with a senior counsel. I was representing a child injured in an automobile accident. I thought the case was worth $5,000. In our settlement discussion, I said that I did not know what it was worth, that my partner had advised me that I could trust this lawyer, and that I was asking him to tell me what it was worth. He said $10,000. I thanked him for his help and accepted it. To make this tactic work, you feign ignorance, ask for help, act humbly and appear grateful if you like the answer.

What do you do if you don't like the answer? You thank the other party for his help and say you must seek instructions. A week later you report back that the client has refused the offer and has instructed you to proceed. This may brand your client as unreasonable but you do not identify yourself with the client. You conclude by saying "he won't settle for less than $15,000". In all probability, you will get more than $5,000. If the worst occurs, before you have to go to trial, you can still retrieve the situation and end up with a reasonable settlement.

CREATING EXPECTATIONS

You should make it clear throughout the negotiations that you expect to do the right thing yourself, you expect your principal to do the right thing, and you certainly expect the other side to do the right thing. You expect a fair and reasonable settlement to be achieved. The desire of people to do the right thing and to live up to the expectations of others is not to be underestimated. If you make it plain that you don't expect much of the other team, because you hold them in low regard and don't expect them to do what is fair and reasonable, the chances are that you won't get much.

14

Closing the Deal

REACHING AN IMPASSE

My experience is that in every negotiation a point of impasse is reached. If you get through it, you have a deal. If you do not, you have a disaster. The reason why every negotiation seems to have an impasse is that both parties want to be satisfied that the well is dry, that they have achieved as much as they can. Impasse implies an end, a willingness to walk away. Reaching and resolving an impasse help to satisfy the concern of both parties that they have gone the last mile in the negotiations.

Therefore, when the impasse arrives, do not despair, for settlement is just around the corner. Do not panic. If you panic, your principal will panic. Do not become aggressive and make promises or threats. You may live to regret these. Simply say to the other party: "Before we break off, let's go back and think about what each of us can do to make this work." You need time for reflection. You need all your imagination and creative skills. You need a clear head. Think. Sleep on it. I have several times found the solutions to impasse in the middle of the night while I was sleeping but my mind was working. Look on it as a challenge that can be conquered, a puzzle that needs a key. Remember that sooner or later there will be a settlement. You can do it sooner. Think. Think. And think some more. You will work it out.

FINDING CREATIVE SOLUTIONS

Finding creative solutions to an impasse in bargaining requires the right attitude and work ethic. First, you must remain optimistic and you must keep your team's optimism at a high level. If everyone gets depressed, nothing good will happen. Second, you must keep the other team involved. If they give up hope, you are finished. Your own optimism and willingness to explore alternatives will prove infectious. Third, you must never stop thinking. Open up your mind. Let it receive all the data. Allow it to work. You will be surprised at what you can come up with.

CONFRONTING YOUR ALTERNATIVES

One way of persuading the other party to move off an impasse is to force it to evaluate the consequences should it refuse to settle now. I call this confronting the reality of your alternatives. Some parties reject a settlement because it is not what they originally wanted or, more likely, had hoped for. But the merits of a settlement must not be judged against a standard of unrealistic expectations. Rather, they must be judged against a standard of what can be achieved if bargaining fails. This is the acid test. I am frequently surprised by the apparent lack of any prior thought on the part of negotiators about the next move, and its consequences, should an impasse occur.

It is rare that negotiations proceed as anticipated. As a result, you never know who it will be who must be forced to confront the reality of the alternatives. It could be you or your counterpart; it could be both. In planning your bargaining objectives, structuring your proposals, and advising your principal, you as a negotiator must always have the next step in mind. What will you do if the negotiations fail? What leverage do you have? How will the public react? Will you be able to win a strike or a lockout? Will you be able to end one if it starts? How will your principal hold up through the stress?

Confronting the reality of one's alternatives involves recognition of the risks implicit in the alternatives. No alternative exists that does not include some risks. The advantage of a settlement is that it offers certainty. It should not take much ingenuity to identify the weaknesses in the other party's professed alternatives—after all, nothing is perfect—and thereby undermine confidence in them. Most people crave certainty.

They would rather settle a dispute than seek confrontation. All they need is an excuse. Give it to them!

Vis-à-vis the other team, there is no obligation to give a balanced assessment of their alternatives. Undermining their confidence through an elaboration of risks is appropriate and will assist you in obtaining a settlement. If you believe that the other side has not been adequately informed by its negotiator of the risks of non-settlement, you can put an offer in writing, combine it with your analysis of the risks of proceeding, and request that it be communicated to the other side's principal.

THE FINAL OFFER

In negotiations, after give-and-take has taken place, a time comes when someone has to say "this is our final offer" and mean it. This stage occurs toward the end of bargaining. When you believe that this point has been reached, you should advise the other party that you are tabling your final position. Do not say it if you do not mean it. The other team will probably not believe you. They will test your resolve. For example, you may offer as your final position an increase of 4%. The other team's last position was 5%. They will try and come back with 4.75%. You should stand firm. They will take it once they are satisfied that they have obtained all that there is. Naturally, until you say "no" and stick to it, you will find it hard to engender a belief that the well is dry.

CLOSING THE DEAL

As a mediator I am frequently told the same thing. No more movement without a guarantee of closure. It is natural to want certainty before giving your bottom line. A mediator can be very helpful in this situation. My practice is to reassure the negotiator that I will not disclose the bottom line unless it buys a deal. I then approach the other negotiator and, with suitable "ifs", "ands", and "buts", determine whether a deal can be made. If it cannot, I try to narrow the differences as much as possible. Sometimes, it takes several trips back and forth, using this technique, to bring both sides to the same point. As a negotiator, you should trust the mediator to "close" the deal for you. If the mediator promises that you won't be sold out, you can rely on it.

If there is no mediator involved, you can achieve the same result by saying to the other negotiator: "I can't get my people to move unless they know that your side will take it. Come back to me with 4% and I will sell it". Where the negotiators trust each other, this is an effective way of closing the deal.

DON'T OVER-REACT

As a negotiator you should be alert to your own principal's reaction when the other party does not eagerly accept your last "very reasonable" offer but counter-offers for a relatively minor improvement. Many people expect to be immediately rewarded for their own reasonableness by an immediate acceptance, without further ado, of their offer. When disappointed, they become resentful and angry. They may want to withdraw their last offer. They may want to start bargaining backwards. Bargaining backwards means making an offer which is worse than your previous offer from the perspective of the other side. It includes such things as increasing your money demand, withdrawing a concession which has not yet been finally signed off, and the like.

You must prevent this disastrous course from being followed. Remind your principal that the other party is merely trying to do the best it can. Talk about human nature; talk about greed. Everybody understands this topic. Tell your principal that you do not have to respond in a positive way to the other side's additional demands, and that you can re-submit your previous offer. This way, everything will work out, and you will demonstrate that you know what you are doing.

"ONE FINAL SQUEEZE"

For some negotiators "one final squeeze" is irresistible. These negotiators are usually insecure. They need to prove to themselves that they got the last drop out of the well. The inherent foolishness of this attitude is that for all they know there may be another drop and another drop. It is all self-delusion. When I negotiate with "squeeze artists", I always have something in reserve. When they squeeze, I give them part of it. They go away happy. If I could trust them, they would have got it all without the squeeze. If you are smart, you won't squeeze.

Indeed, there is a slight risk that the "final squeeze" may cost you the settlement because the other side will be so angered that it will back off completely. More often, you will end up settling for what was already there. But even if you get a bit more, in the long term the squeeze play will hurt your credibility.

THE DEAL IS MADE

After the deal is made, restrain any ecstatic reactions. These will only upset the other party. On the other hand, acting like a sourpuss will also not improve the relationship. Congratulate your own team, thank them for their help, and congratulate your counterpart. Try to remove any bitterness which may have developed in the heat of battle.

And do not forget to pat yourself on the back for having achieved a fair and reasonable settlement. Never worry or criticize yourself for what you did not achieve. Focus on the positive!

15

Mediation and Fact-Finding

THE USE OF MEDIATORS

The use of mediators to resolve disputes is becoming increasingly popular. They are used in commercial disputes, neighbourhood disputes, family disputes, environmental disputes and just about every kind of dispute that you can think of. Even judges are attempting to act as mediators at pre-trial conferences. There are, of course, mediators in labour disputes. Some days, it seems that everybody wants to be a mediator.

Of course, mediation has long been used to settle labour disputes, and it is very likely that in your negotiations you will resort to mediation yourself. Some words of definition are, therefore, appropriate.

A "conciliator" tries to persuade the parties to settle their disputes, but has no power to decide anything. A "mediator" is another name for a conciliator. Although they have no more power than conciliators, mediators like to think of themselves as more "high powered" than conciliators. A "fact-finder" is a neutral third party who is commissioned to write a report about a dispute and to make recommendations for settlement. Neither the report nor the recommendations are binding.

Sometimes various roles are combined. For example, a "mediator-arbitrator" is a person who adjudicates the dispute if he or she fails to persuade the parties to settle it voluntarily.

MED-ARB

Some people give me credit for popularizing mediation-arbitration in Ontario. This process, referred to as "med-arb", allows one to mediate and, if mediation fails, arbitrate the dispute. But the fact is that I have reservations about med-arb. It is precisely because I have no power to force the parties to do anything that I feel free as a mediator to put pressure on them, by confronting each side with the reality, i.e. shortcomings, of its alternatives.

If you pressure parties as a mediator when you are also the arbitrator, it makes the arbitration appear a foregone conclusion. Yet in any adjudicative process it is essential not only that justice be done, but that it be seen to be done. The arbitrator must appear to be impartial if the parties are to feel that they have been fairly treated. It is impossible for an overactive mediator-arbitrator to maintain the appearance of neutrality in any particular dispute. It is for this very reason that judges who mediate at pre-trial conferences are not permitted to conduct the trial.

However there are some advantages to "med-arb". It allows the arbitrator to find out during the mediation process the parties' priorities, and to plumb their bottom line. In this way, mistakes can be avoided, such as giving the wrong benefit, awarding too much or too little, or exceeding the range of the reasonable. These mistakes can be costly.

TROIKA MEDIATION

Sometimes there is an advantage in having a "troika" mediate, i.e. two nominees of the parties and an independent chairperson. The nominees of the parties can do much of the negotiating, while consulting the parties who appointed them, and protect the mediator from over-use. Differences can be resolved with the assistance of the mediator when matters become tense or difficult. In my opinion, nothing works as well as an independent chair with partisan nominees, if all three know what they are doing, and are committed to finding a win-win solution. Two good negotiators and a mediator are effectively the same thing as a three-member mediation team. However, the negotiators must both be experienced and effective, trust each other and have confidence in the mediator. Without that, the process cannot work. This is something to consider the next time you need some help.

BARGAINING WITH MEDIATION IN MIND

You have to plan for the presence of a neutral at the *outset of your negotiations*. In other words, you ought to consider whether or not the dispute can be settled without the assistance of a mediator. If you conclude before the negotiations start that a settlement is unlikely, prior to mediation, then you should structure your bargaining on the basis that you will keep something to give away at mediation.

From my own perspective, this approach makes me much more effective as a mediator, because I can then elicit concessions in mediation that the other party was unable to achieve in negotiations. The danger with this approach is that it may preclude in advance any possibility of settlement in face-to-face bargaining prior to mediation. The negotiator must weigh the risks. If you keep something in your pocket, you may get a deal at mediation; but you may also make an early settlement impossible, when a deal could be made at the table. And mediation involves delay which can be prejudicial.

There are two schools of thought on this subject: one school believes that the best deal is one the parties make themselves, and that a settlement made in direct negotiations is the sign of a mature relationship. I endorse this approach since it entails acceptance by the parties of responsibility for their own affairs. But another school of negotiators, who wish to avoid responsibility for the result, welcome the involvement of a neutral whom they can blame. "He made me do it" is a not infrequent justification for a settlement. Negotiators who adopt this approach use the mediator as a means of levering their principal into a settlement. The mediator acts as the ritual scapegoat.

If you are satisfied that there will be no settlement until a mediator has been appointed, it is pointless for you to give away too much during the negotiation, as the mediator will need items to trade off in order to drive bargaining in the direction of a settlement. A mediator expects that you will not have given everything up before the mediation begins, and will be very annoyed if it turns out that you have nothing more to give.

One of the ground rules of bargaining is that any offers that are exchanged between the parties are made "without prejudice" and cannot be disclosed to a third party, such as a mediator. Do not delude yourself that you can rely on this understanding. Although everyone agrees that offers will be "without prejudice", no one pays more than lip service to the principle. A mediator will be told by someone what the positions were in bargaining. Therefore, if you have offered 5% in the bargaining and it has not brought you a deal, there is no point telling the mediator that your position is 3%. The other side will tell the mediator privately what the truth is. A proposal made with or without prejudice is a horse that has escaped from the barn.

If you are persuaded at the outset that the dispute will likely not settle until a mediator is involved, it is better to disclose this frankly to the other side. Sit down with the other negotiator, present your own position, make it clear that you do not want to waste time, that you do not want the other team to make concessions on the basis that they will be reciprocated, when they won't, and that you would like their co-operation in obtaining the assistance of a neutral. There will be less likelihood that your relationship with the other party will deteriorate if you are candid than if you make a half-hearted pretence at serious negotiating.

FACE TO FACE MEETINGS

Joint meetings offer a number of advantages which I suspect many negotiators are not aware of. For one thing, if points are discussed directly across the table, it saves the time that would otherwise be spent by the mediator and the negotiators in travelling backwards and forwards from room to room. Another important advantage is that it avoids exaggeration and misunderstandings. With one party absent, the other party feels less inhibited in asserting points which may be only partly true or which may have no foundation except in fantasy. Face to face meetings of both sides restrain unwarranted assertions, and prevent misunderstandings.

No one wants to be made a fool of in public. A good mediator can be merciless if there are repeated departures from a reasonable standard of accuracy. Direct encounters also permit a mediator to suggest compromises which are frequently accepted at the table. The negotiators themselves may suggest a compromise assuming they have the permission of their principals in advance. Momentum can soon develop and progress can be made quickly. Face to face meetings help to restore the parties' confidence in their own ability to communicate with each other. If the parties learn to improve their communication skills, they will enhance their relationship and require less assistance in the future.

On the other hand, the relationship between the parties may be so toxic that separate sessions with the mediator are necessary. In these circumstances, the mediator must be careful to maintain confidences while at the same time checking with the parties where there are contrary assertions.

SIZING UP THE MEDIATOR

In some jurisdictions, mediation or conciliation services are supplied by the government, and the parties have no control over the selection of the individual who will be available. But if you have a say in who the neutral is going to be, you will want to choose a mediator who knows how to mediate. Some suggestions may be in order on how to deal with both situations.

So far as I know, there are no training programs for people who wish to practise as mediators, despite the fact that acting as a mediator is the most difficult of all neutral roles in labour relations, and one which requires the greatest skill and experience. If you end up with a mediator who does not know how to mediate, my suggestion is to ignore the mediator, and try to settle the matter yourselves. It is your football and the mediator cannot spoil your game if you do not allow it. If you let an incompetent mediator intervene in your dispute, you may end up in an impasse from which there may be no escape.

A number of years ago I appeared before a judge of wide experience who knew nothing about mediation. At a pre-trial conference, designed to promote a settlement, this judge told the other party at the outset that, if it were up to him, he would not offer more than $50,000 to settle the action. Fortunately, the other lawyer was more sensible, and we settled the case for three times the amount that the judge had suggested. As a general rule, mediators should not express an opinion which is contrary to the interests of one party in the presence of the other party. All this accomplishes is to polarize the parties. One side becomes set in its position; the other side becomes defensive, and seeks to argue the point. The proper role of mediators is privately to expose to each side the weaknesses in its position, so that both parties can better confront the reality of their alternatives. There are no negotiations without risks. Emphasizing the risks induces a cooperative attitude.

The first sign that the mediator is not likely to be very helpful is a demonstrated inability to take charge of the proceedings. Apart from those cases where there has been no bargaining, a mediator arrives on the scene after the parties have been unsuccessful in their own approach to the resolution of the dispute. Accordingly, the mediator should feel free to determine the agenda, establish the ground rules, and get on with the mediation.

The mediator must be able to mediate, i.e. generate the give-and-take of bargaining. If the mediator functions only as a messenger between the negotiating teams, you know that you have an incompetent neutral on your hands. Very likely, even the messages will be garbled. Have nothing to do with such a mediator.

An effective mediator will want to spend time finding out what the positions of the parties are, with a view to assisting them in their bargaining. When the mediator wants to spend a lot of time learning about the intricacies of the workplace, you are in trouble. The experts in the workplace are the parties, not the mediator. All the mediator needs to know is: What is the nature of the problems that a particular party is experiencing? What solution does that party want? Does the solution create a difficulty for the other party? This can be accomplished across the table in a relatively short time. A mediator who is busy learning about the workplace, travelling around, and interviewing personnel is a mediator who will never settle anything. Let this mediator travel while you stay and bargain.

Another indication that a mediator is not likely to be helpful is a desire on the mediator's part to solve all your drafting problems. It is not, in my opinion, the job of the mediator to draft clauses for the parties. Drafting should be done by those who have to live with the language. Only if there is a stumbling block in drafting is it appropriate for a mediator to make a suggestion to help resolve a difficulty.

DEALING WITH THE MEDIATOR

How should you behave toward a competent mediator? Co-operate fully. The effective mediator will help you make a settlement and will not give your position away without getting something back in return. A good mediator will not sell you out, will not hang you out to dry. If a deal is not in the cards, the mediator will let you know quickly. This does not mean that the competent mediator will act as a sympathetic security blanket. You can expect the competent mediator to be frank with you and tell you about the risks you face, but you can be confident that the same is being done with the other side. Best of all, good mediators have creative ideas for settling problems.

It is important, however, to recognize that there is a limit to how many things one person can sell to another person, no matter how competent. Aluminum siding salespeople do not sell televisions. You must do the minor selling yourself. That is to say, you must sell your own principal on the relatively insignificant items in the dispute. When you come to the crunch, if the mediator can help you sell something which you are unable to sell, then by all means ask for help. My own practice is never to go behind the professional negotiator unless I am asked to do so. I do not want to become overly involved with the principals because there is a risk of crossed signals and mixed messages. In any event, you do not want to use up the limited stock of credibility that a mediator possesses to sell the other side on items that are relatively insignificant.

As a mediator, I do not object to being blamed for positions which the negotiators themselves want their principals to accept. This is part of the process. It is an unwritten understanding. The mediator must be prepared to serve as the scapegoat if necessary, even if it makes one *persona non grata* in the future. However, if you blame the mediator, bear in mind that a sophisticated principal may wonder why you yourself are not more effective. Nevertheless, from time to time this tactic can prove very useful.

Many people expect that the mediator will do everything for them and there is nothing left for them to do. This is a mistake. Mediators can only assist in making a settlement. They can move the matter along but the work still has to be done by the parties; it is the parties who have to make the decisions. The responsibility to "bite the bullet" belongs to the parties, not the mediator. No one ever successfully mediated a dispute where the parties were not ready to reach a settlement. The mediator can bring the parties to water, but cannot force them to drink.

In my opinion, a mediator has no business trying to get the exact deal the mediator thinks is right. There is a wide range of acceptable results in any given set of negotiations. Let the parties find their own "perfect" result. After all, they have to live with it. I will intervene only if I observe a party about to make a catastrophic blunder which will hurt the relationship in the future. Bargaining is not about windfalls. In rare cases, in public sector disputes, I consider it proper to intervene if it is clear that the proposed tentative agreement will not be ratified by one or other of the parties. The deleterious effects of non-ratification in an on-going relationship entitle a mediator to take this drastic course. I believe, in a limited way, that the mediator must protect the public interest.

Let me give you an example. Years ago, I mediated a dispute between teachers and a school board in a small county in south-western Ontario. A strike had been underway for a number of weeks, but the trustees who voted to sustain a strike found that their enthusiasm diminished as the strike progressed. Why? Because the parents became increasingly annoyed as their children remained out of school and they began calling the trustees at all hours of the day and night, threatening to vote them out of office in the next election unless classes quickly resumed. The trustees became anxious to settle and, by the time I entered the scene as mediator, they were willing to give away the store in order to end the strike. I cautioned them against making a settlement that would cause them to develop a "get even" attitude in the next round of bargaining.

However, although I do not share this view entirely, mediators generally take the position that the quality of settlements is none of their business. It is not the job of a mediator to hand-hold a party, at a time of great pressure, in order to prevent it from making a bad deal. As a negotiator, this is your job.

CONFRONTING REALITIES

As a mediator, when I am faced with a party who is being unreasonable, I usually proceed as follows. I make it plain that I do not expect anyone who has a better alternative to settle. Why should a party settle now if it can do measurably better by waiting? I then ask the bargaining team what their next step is. After they tell me, we have a discussion about how realistic their expectations are as to the likely result.

In the course of this discussion, I may criticize their assumptions; I may emphasize the risks. If a trial looms, I point out the differences in the attitudes of judges and the prohibition against judge-shopping. If an arbitration hearing lies ahead, I may advert to a known disposition of the arbitrator which is unfavourable to their position. If we are discussing a strike or lockout, I would alert the party to the pressures that they would be under to cave in after a three or four-week strike. If one individual is obstructing a settlement, I remind this person that in my experience there is usually a victim at the end of every strike, someone who can be blamed for the mess. Don't be that victim, I warn. In one case, in which I delivered this message, it fell upon deaf ears; after the strike was settled, this individual ended up in a remote location.

MAKING PUBLIC RECOMMENDATIONS

A mediator can sometimes assist in achieving a settlement by making recommendations. Indeed, in public sector disputes the negotiators may prefer to have a mediator's proposal than to agree to a settlement themselves, even one to which they have no real objection. Why? Because this allows their principals, usually politicians, to assume less responsibility. They can argue that they did not have much choice. It's a case of "blame the mediator". In these circumstances the deal is actually struck in advance, although packaged as a mediator's proposal. Any mediator will co-operate in stage-managing such a scenario.

More controversial is a mediator's proposal which does not have prior acceptance, but is advanced by the mediator for the purpose of encouraging a settlement. It may include a detailed rationale for the proposed settlement. I have used this form of proposal in public sector disputes in which the community takes an active interest. This tactic permits the mediator to appeal directly to the parties' constituencies. If the public accepts the proposal, the negotiators will not be far behind. Additionally, the proposal stands as a written record of what might have been achievable without a strike or lockout. If confrontation does not produce more, the negotiators will not be able to explain away a poor result. Nothing motivates people, especially politicians, more than the prospect or fear of accountability. To encourage responsibility, a price must be exacted for irresponsibility.

Rarely should a mediator publicly adopt the final offer of one of the parties. This is a course of action which I do not recommend. On one occasion, in a public sector dispute which attracted considerable media attention, the negotiator for the employer asked me to publicly endorse his final offer. While I considered the offer a reasonable one, I replied that I would endorse it only if the employer would guarantee that it would not improve the offer if the union refused to accept it. As I expected, this assurance was not forthcoming, for politicians will not, and probably ought not to, tie their hands. Indeed, it was likely that the union could get more, and there was no reason to stand in its way by endorsing a final offer which was likely not final.

A mediator can be embarrassed by taking a party at its word when it claims to have offered "all there is". For example, in one major public sector dispute, the fact-finder recommended the employer's final offer. He had been assured by the politicians that no more money was available. When the employees refused to accept the recommendation, guess what? The employer promptly offered more! A mediator's career is not enhanced by such incidents.

FACT-FINDING

Fact-finders are persons who are required to make a report with recommendations for settlement. Usually, they will first try to mediate a settlement. They are found in the education sector in Ontario. Under federal legislation, and in other jurisdictions, they are called conciliation boards.

Fact-finding is a difficult neutral role to perform successfully. Unlike arbitrators who can bring finality to a dispute, or mediators who ordinarily do not make public reports, fact-finders issue non-binding reports with recommendations. Instead of promoting settlements, these recommendations, if not carefully considered, can polarize the parties and impair the chances of a successful resolution of the dispute. I recall one situation in which I was asked to mediate after a fact-finding report. The fact-finder recommended a 5-6% increase. In reality, because of other settlements, 6% was the right amount. The union would not take less. However, the employer felt it would look foolish if it settled at 6%, since the fact-finder had recommended a range of 5-6%. If the fact-finder had recommended 6%, there would not have been a problem. Only after intensive mediation was I able to persuade the parties to reach an agreement at 5.95% and avoid a strike.

When a fact-finder wants to mediate, make sure that what you say in confidence during the mediation does not end up in the report. Otherwise, if there is no settlement, and your "bottom line" is exposed in the report, you will have nothing left for bargaining, or for the next neutral who arrives on the scene. My advice is this. If the fact-finder wants to mediate, ask for an assurance that there will be no recommendations if settlement is not achieved in the mediation.

16

Arbitration and Final Offer Selection

INTEREST ARBITRATION

Arbitrators are like judges, in the sense that they have the power to decide the issues in dispute. Their decisions are binding on the parties. However, whereas "rights" arbitrators decide disputes arising out of contracts, "interest" arbitrators, or boards of arbitration, make the contract for the parties by determining wages and working conditions.

Interest arbitration boards usually consist of three members: the chairperson and nominees appointed by each of the parties. Where the arbitration board is unable to achieve unanimity, the award of the majority will govern; if there is no majority, the award of the chairperson will prevail.

Negotiators in public sector disputes, where arbitration is often the ultimate dispute resolution mechanism, must fully understand the interest arbitration process if they want to perform their duties as negotiators effectively. Interest arbitration is not a process of adjudicating rights and wrongs, but is part of the continuum of collective bargaining. For this reason, most interest arbitrators try to achieve a consensual result by mediating between the parties' nominees. Nominees are, indeed, vital to the success of interest arbitration. They are aware of the parties' priorities, and their "bottom line" positions. They will usually prevent a well-meaning arbitrator from straying too far from the range of reasonable.

FINAL OFFER SELECTION

This is "Russian roulette" arbitration. The arbitrator chooses one offer or the other, either on a package or on an issue-by-issue basis, and has no power to chart a middle course. The theory of final offer selection is that each side will be stimulated to move toward a reasonable position, out of fear that otherwise the arbitrator will prefer the other side's offer. Sometimes it works. If both packages are in the range of the reasonable, it makes no difference which offer the arbitrator selects. Unfortunately, as has happened in the past, both packages may be unreasonable. In this case, whichever offer is selected, you have a big winner, a big loser, and serious problems in the future. Avoid final offer selection unless, perhaps, it is combined with mediation. The mediator, if the dispute is not settled, is likely to persuade the parties to moderate their packages sufficiently so that they fall within a reasonable range.

I hold the same opinion of "final offer selection" even when conducted on an issue-by-issue basis. Theoretically, this approach poses less risk. The selector has some discretion in fashioning the overall award. Realistically, however, wages will likely be the crucial issue. If the parties are far apart on wages at the time of the selection, then the process will have failed. To repeat, you cannot count on the process forcing the parties to be reasonable. It is in those cases where reasonableness is most required that it is least likely to be found.

ABILITY TO PAY

An issue which plagues interest arbitration is the relevance of an employer's ability to afford a wage increase. While the ability of the employer to pay is relevant in the private sector, there is neither academic nor arbitral support in Canada for the relevance of ability to pay in public sector disputes. Yet, despite the virtual unanimity among experts and professionals, there is a perennial hue and cry, particularly from politicians, over the insufficiency of criteria in the statutes which provide for compulsory binding arbitration in public sector wage disputes in Ontario. Indeed, some politicians consider that they are softening their periodic attacks on arbitrators by suggesting that the errors into which we have fallen would have been prevented if we had the guidance of appropriate criteria, particularly "ability to pay". It is this criterion which is closest to their hearts, and which is raised invariably at any seminar or conference at which public sector employers are present.

Arbitrators have rejected "ability to pay" as a relevant criterion in public sector interest arbitrations almost from the outset. For example, in one case, Judge Anderson stated:

> "An arbitrator should not make decisions based on budgetary limitations and priorities set by the government, otherwise he would not be completely independent as he must always be."
>
> [referred to in *Ryerson Polytechnical Institute* (1973), 4 L.A.C. (2d) 9 (Brown)]

In another case, Arbitrator Shime put the matter as follows:

> "Public sector employees should not be required to subsidize the community by accepting substandard wages and

working conditions ... On balance, the total community which requires the service should shoulder the financial loss and not expect the employees of the industry to bear an unfair burden by accepting wages and working conditions which are substandard ... If the community needs and demands the public service, then the members of the community must bear the necessary cost to provide fair and equitable wages and not expect the employees to subsidize the service by accepting substandard wages."

> [*British Columbia Ry. Co.*, unreported,
> June 1, 1976, at p.8]

Subsequently, Arbitrator Adams stated:

"[To base wages on ability to pay] would force employees to subsidize these services to the public and render interest arbitration under the Hospital Labour Disputes Arbitration Act largely irrelevant. Terms and conditions of employment would be unilaterally determined by the Government during the budgeting process."

> [*Central Park Lodges*, unreported,
> June 25, 1982, at p.38]

Although I agree with these comments, I want to add some thoughts of my own. The principal problem that I have always found with the "ability to pay" argument in the public sector is that in truth it is not, in the ordinary sense of the words, a matter of ability to pay. Public sector employers always have the "ability to pay" through the use of the taxing power directly or indirectly. In the public sector, "ability to pay" means simply that the employer, for reasons which are often political, does not *want* to pay. Politicians do not want to raise taxes or cut services or lay off employees. However, although no one is in favour of raising taxes or of cutting services or of laying off employees, these are the difficult political choices which politicians are elected to make.

On the other hand, in the private sector, there is real meaning to the expression "ability to pay". One can determine objectively by an examination of the employer's balance sheet what the employer's ability to pay is and what the impact of any proposed settlement might be on the company's profitability.

In its "wage restraint" legislation, in the 1980's, the Ontario government tied "ability to pay" to "existing provincial fiscal policy", and also made it clear that five per cent was "existing provincial fiscal policy". In my opinion, this was a direct interference with the independence of arbitrators and an attempt to impose not only a criterion but a specific result. In effect, the government sought to "use" the criterion of "ability to pay" to its own advantage.

For my own part, although I refused to work under this legislation, I would have been quite willing to work under a statute which required that we take into account freely negotiated private sector and public sector settlements to the extent these reflected the economic conditions within the community. But, arbitrators cannot, consistent with their own independence, be pressured directly or indirectly into implementing government fiscal policy, particularly where it has not been adopted in freely negotiated settlements within the private or the public sector.

While fiscal restraint is a worthwhile objective, it cannot be achieved by misusing the concept of "ability to pay" so as to deprive the parties of a truly fair and independent process of arbitration. Independent arbitrators are essential to any system which has deprived parties of the usual right to strike or lock out. Moreover, criteria can be developed which are consistent with the independence of arbitrators. Such criteria would emphasize the need for taking into account the economic conditions within the community in fashioning wage awards.

COMPARABLE SETTLEMENTS

The principal value of a freely negotiated settlement is not that an arbitrated settlement is likely to be less fair from an objective point of view. Rather, it is better that the parties who have to live with the results be responsible for the choices. The parties will accept and respect the contracts they make in preference to the contracts that others make for them.

Arbitrators are, of course, neither the instruments of government policies nor do they, in any meaningful sense, fashion policy. Once one assumes that employees in the public sector should receive wages and benefits which are neither more nor less than those paid to employees in comparable positions in the private sector, the private sector response to economic conditions within the community provides the essential guidepost for arbitrators to follow in resolving public sector disputes. Therefore, although I reject "ability to pay" as a criterion in public sector disputes, I believe that we must follow the private sector's response to economic conditions within the community as reflected in its wage settlements.

Some years ago, in determining the wage increase for Windsor firefighters, immediately prior to Ontario's wage restraint legislation, I attempted to explain my position as to how economic conditions within the community should be reflected by arbitrators. I trust that I will be forgiven for quoting extensively from this award:

> "Mr. Brode seems of the opinion that I had invented or originated the principle that ability to pay in a public sector dispute is not relevant. In fact, Justice Emmett Hall is usually credited with the observation. In any event, the principle has become so well-established that one rarely finds counsel for

employers even raising it in a public sector dispute. That is not to say that counsel do not draw the economic conditions in a community to our attention or that arbitrators are insensitive to or ignore the economic climate within which their awards have application. What has happened in Windsor, unfortunately, is that attention was focused only on one passage of my award, and the rest was apparently ignored. The rest is important because it is expressly recognized that there is an appropriate basis for taking adverse economic conditions within a community into account; namely, if the evidence discloses that the community generally has moderated its wage expectations, then an interest arbitrator should reflect that moderation in his award, and should reflect moderation to the extent that the community is showing restraint. Arbitrators must do this because, although public sector employees are not required to subsidize the community by accepting substandard wages and benefits, the community is not required to pay greater wages or benefits to public sector employees than the community itself is able to derive from its employment.

The difficulty with the ability to pay argument in its simple form is that public sector employers ordinarily do have the ability to pay. The City of Windsor clearly has such ability in this particular case. The fact, however, that the City of Windsor has the ability to pay 15%, as requested, is no reason to award 15%. As I have said, what an interest arbitrator must do is determine what the community generally is obtaining by way of wage settlements and must take that fact into account as a relevant consideration in determining an appropriate salary increase."

[*City of Windsor*, unreported, September 17, 1982]

The fact is that, in all respects, arbitrators attempt to emulate the results of free collective bargaining. As I noted in an award involving the City of Ottawa police: "Interest arbitrators interpret the collective bargaining scene. They do not sit in judgment of its results." If arbitrators' awards are considered inflationary or too high or otherwise unsatisfactory, it is ordinarily because freely negotiated settlements both in the private and in the public sector are inflationary, too high or otherwise unsatisfactory.

One should remember that the vast majority of settlements achieved in Canada are voluntary settlements in which an interest arbitrator has no part. This observation is true even in those sectors which are controlled by compulsory binding arbitration. The reality is that the parties conveniently forget their own freely negotiated settlements, whereas they are quick to criticize arbitrators whose awards simply mirror these settlements. Nevertheless, these settlements must be followed because the goal of compulsory binding arbitration is to ensure that employees affected by the loss of the right to strike fare as well, although no better than, employees whose settlements are negotiated within the customary framework of the right to strike and lock out.

The parties in public sector disputes seem reluctant to "bite the bullet" and to "make deals". It is possible for them to avoid taking responsibility because in many public sector disputes a breakdown in negotiations results in an arbitration, not in a strike or lockout. An arbitration does not seem as bad as a strike or a lockout. No one loses any wages. Service to the public is not interrupted. And, most importantly, a party who makes a deal risks criticism whereas the party who refuses to settle can criticize the other party for making settlement impossible and denounce the arbitrator for making a stupid decision, if dissatisfied with the award.

Persuading a party who has the right to arbitrate that a voluntary settlement is better is no easy task. You must find a way to undermine the other side's belief that proceeding to arbitration is less threatening personally than a settlement would be. If all else fails, appeal to the other side's sense of responsibility. Sometimes it works.

NON-RATIFIED SETTLEMENTS

Negotiators in public sector disputes sometimes make tentative agreements which are not ratified. I suspect that the failure to ratify in part results from the belief that one may be able to get more at arbitration, and the worst that can happen is that the arbitrator will simply enforce the non-ratified settlement. It is generally thought that there is no risk of getting less. This is not my view. In one award I expressed my opinion as follows:

> "It must always be remembered that offers of settlement are 'without prejudice' until actual agreement is reached. An arbitrator has no interest in such offers. They should not be disclosed to him and any attempt to prejudice a party by referring to such an offer of settlement is improper. Until the parties ratify the tentative agreement, there is no agreement. If ratification does not occur then the parties are free to adopt any negotiating posture they choose.
>
> It is, of course, very unfortunate when tentative agreements are not ratified but the failure to ratify when the negotiating committee has in good faith recommended the settlement, is not bargaining in bad faith nor should it be cause for exacerbating tensions between the parties. It must be understood that there is always a chance that ratification may not take place. Parties who have offered to settle are protected by law in the event ratification does not occur because the offer they have made may not subsequently be used against them. They are neither legally nor morally bound to renew the offer. The party who declines to ratify must not and cannot expect that the offer once refused remains open as a minimum base from which he may negotiate upward."
>
> [*Ottawa Board of Education*, unreported,
> August 24, 1977]

I elaborated on this point in a subsequent award:

"[I]n my opinion, a tentative agreement is no more than the opinion of the negotiating teams as to what is reasonable. I do not think that any arbitrator would permit such evidence of the opinion of members of the negotiating team to be given orally. That the opinion is a mutual one and reduced to writing does not add to its probative value. In disputes which are tried in our courts, tentative agreements between counsel which are not accepted by their principals (when it is known that counsel has no authority to bind his client) are inadmissible. These are part of the negotiating process and are protected by the 'without prejudice' privilege. This privilege is designed to encourage parties to settle. I am not aware of, nor has any reason been suggested to me, of any special circumstance peculiar to the labour relations context which justifies a departure from the usual rule. It is a serious infringement on the right of a principal to reject his agent's advice if that agent's advice is admitted in evidence and given weight.

Parties who reject tentative agreements and proceed to arbitration should not ... fear the adoption of the settlement by the board of arbitration. Rather, they should fear a different result, one which may be worse than the settlement they have rejected. As the matter now stands, if the employees reject the settlement, they may get more at arbitration but they will not get less. As far as I am concerned, this is an unsatisfactory dynamic and obviously one which encourages rejection. On the other hand, if the negotiating team were to advise the membership that rejection may be followed by an adverse result at arbitration, the situation could well be different. Similarly, as matters now stand, an employer, particularly in the public sector, can reject a settlement, proceed to arbitration and be assured that the result will not be worse than the tentative settlement. This facilitates their avoiding taking responsibility for decision making. In my opinion, the very evil which the present rule of admitting tentative, non-ratified agreements into evidence is designed to avoid, namely, rejection of the settlements by the principals, is, in fact, exacerbated by the rule. Accordingly, as a matter of policy, it would be preferable not to admit these matters into evidence, quite apart from the fact that as a matter of law I think they are not admissible."

> [*Peel Board of Education*, unreported,
> May 4, 1981]

It seems to me that the attitudes of arbitrators on this issue have changed, and that my view now reflects the prevailing approach. However, some arbitrators still take non-ratified settlements into account, and parties should make them explicitly "without prejudice" if they wish to be sure that the settlement will not return to haunt them at arbitration.

CONCLUSION

You will be a successful negotiator if you have a thorough knowledge of the subject-matter, obtain a sensible mandate from your principals, make an effective presentation of your demands, and adopt a win/win approach to negotiations.

Books are guides. If they give you an idea or two, they are worth reading. But nothing can replace thinking. It is a good idea to think more, and read less, even if the latter is easier. Apply your creativity, your imagination and your intelligence to the negotiations at hand. All the answers lie in *your* head and in *your* heart.

You can do it!